More Cee Dub's
Dutch Oven
and Other Camp Cookin'

Spiced with *More* Tall Tales

By C. W. "Butch" Welch

Back Country Press
Penny L. Welch, Publish~

Copyright © 2000 by C. W. "Butch" W~

ALL RIGHTS RESERVED. No part of this book may be reproduced without the express written consent of the publisher, except in the case of brief excerpts in critical reviews and articles. All inquiries should be addressed to Back Country Press, P.O. Box 190, Grangeville, Idaho 83530. Email: bcpress@ceedubs.com.

Printed in the United States of America
First Printing - 2000
Second Printing - 2001
Third Printing - 2002

Computer Graphics - Gary Mitchell

ISBN # 0-96726472-3

DEDICATION

TO

HANK KETCHIE

RICH RODGERS

GREG ROST

BILL HOSKINS

&

SNOOSE

Campfire conversation! Dinner is done, the Dutch ovens are cleaned up and it's time to throw another log on the fire. A time to recount the day's adventures or just swap yarns and enjoy one another's company. Read the journals of the free trappers and mountain men who explored the West in the early 1800's and you'll see how even they cherished conversation and companionship at day's end. Many a night my only company was my old Black Lab. In selecting stories to include in this book, my thoughts turned to five pardners, one of them canine, who are no longer around to share a campfire. To their memory I dedicate this book.

C.W. "BUTCH" WELCH

'The Big Cabin'
Bartlett-Hopkins Ranch
South Fork of Clearwater River
Grangeville, Idaho
March 2000

Table of Contents

Butch with IGBS - Bear No. 1. Cap and Ball Park, Lodgepole Creek, Wyoming. June, 1977. C.W. Welch Photo Collection

ACKNOWLEDGEMENTS

I didn't realize how many folks it takes to produce a book until I myself started writing with the purpose of publishing. It's my name that shows up on the Library of Congress catalog card but without the assistance, input, and support of many others it couldn't happen! It is impossible to name and acknowledge everyone who contributed to this book. Some contributions were inadvertent and I take sole responsibility for the portrayal of events involving the actions of others and me. However, as I told one person who seems to find himself the subject of my writing on frequent occasions, he can write a book if he wants the story told from his perspective! Anyway…

Thanks go to all the camp cooks who graciously shared recipes. Their unselfishness is the reader's reward! I also want to thank my folks, Buzz and Betty, and my sisters, Julia, Carol, and Debbie for their support, encouragement and ideas. Cecil and Cora Earp of CanyonView Ranch, Grangeville, Idaho, deserve special thanks not only for their friendship but also for sharing their view of Cottonwood Creek displayed on the front cover.

In 1971 I began working for the Idaho Department of Fish & Game as a Biological Aide. I went on to work as a Conservation Officer from 1978-1999. Talk about camping opportunities! I wore out more sleeping bags than I care to remember, but the friends I made and the experiences I gained, cannot be purchased anywhere at any cost. Besides being great to work for and with, Al Nicholson, Brent Hyde, Don Wright, Tom Lucia, and Brent Nyborg, never complained about a grocery bill and always came back for second helpings! I would be remiss if I didn't include "extra special thanks" to Sue Nass, the producer of *Incredible Idaho*. I value her friendship, support, and insight, along with her contributing the *Foreword*.

My river companions, Tom and Bill Beck, Dan Miller (aka 'No Class'), Mike McLain, Harold Bergman, Don and Kris Van Cleave, John Nagel, and Dave McGonigal. Besides recipes, they have contributed friendship, support, and perspective. Jim Van Ark, who took the back cover photo, fits in this category as well. Credit for the cover photo goes to Roy Kinner, a friend and former co-worker.

Thanks also go to our printer, Ron Morris, of Joslyn & Morris, Inc., and his employees Heidi Buffi and Bob Stauts for their advice, patience, and experience. Also, Gary Mitchell contributed his technical expertise to get this project to the printer.

When I found myself being unwillingly thrust into the computer era, I experienced frequent bouts of cyber panic! My stepson, Matt Dykas, continues to answer the phone, my questions, and share his knowledge. I'll be forever in his debt. Thanks also go to my son, Brian, for all his help lugging Dutch ovens, washing dishes, cleaning equipment, and doing whatever I ask! His sense of humor has bailed us both out on occasion.

The person who deserves the greatest thanks is my publisher, editor, chief slicer and dicer, worthy Scrabble opponent, hunting pardner, best friend, and wife, Penny! Thanks, Babe!

PS: Thanks to Steve Pratt for loaning me a hat for the cover photo!

FOREWORD

From game warden to gourmet. . .just when you think you have Cee Dub figured out something will surprise you, like this career change. I never thought he would leave the life of a game warden. Where will he get his material? It was the source of endless stories always told with self-depreciating humor and a twinkle in the eye. Each story inevitably began, "I knew this 'ole' boy back in . . . ." Usually they ended in raucous laughter. But, sometimes you'd see the other side of Butch, the quiet afterward, when the story is about an old friend who now runs rivers in another world.

Being a game warden in Idaho is a tough job. It is big country, with isolated areas tucked into breathtaking wilderness. You get around Idaho's back country by mule, by horse, by foot or by running the rivers in rafts. And protecting the state's wildlife from poachers has its own element of danger in country so remote. I spent many a trip with Butch as the writer/producer of a wildlife show, and I salute his perseverance, his integrity, his faith in himself and his natural ability to tell a story. The wild world is a better place because of Butch.

What will I miss? I will miss his good nature when things go wrong. I will miss his sardonic humor. I will miss his blatant irreverence for rules imposed by small minds. I will miss his professionalism and sense of responsibility. It was always there underneath, mixing the demands of the job with the need for all of us to enjoy our work.

I will miss his penchant for the classic, romantic story. Is there anyone who can tell the tales of the Salmon River settlers with such obvious affection, respect, and wonder? Maybe he was one of them in another life.

And of course, I will miss Butch's Dutch oven cooking! A river trip with Butch Welch becomes a study in contrasts. Savory gourmet meals emerge hot and steaming from clumsy black cauldrons called Dutch ovens. A delicate, dry white wine appears accompanied by one of Butch's tall tales better suited to rot-gut rum. And after hoots of laughter with the main course, Butch quietly offers a simple toast to old and absent friends before serving up slices of Dutch oven-delicious pineapple upside down cake. . .all beneath the velvet star-studded skies of Idaho's wilderness.

Now the whole nation will get to taste a bit of Butch's best. See you out there!

Sue Nass, Television Writer/Producer <u>Incredible Idaho</u>.

INTRODUCTION

If one thinks about it, Camp Cookin' dates back to the beginning of time. For those early campers grub meant survival. They weren't concerned about quality nearly as much as quantity and if there was enough to last through the next day. My best guess is folks spent the better part of their waking hours searching for grub while looking over their shoulders making sure some critter wasn't intent on converting them into a meal! In this day and age a camper unfortunately must worry more about other humans than wild critters.

Today's camper merely checks out a book from the library to determine which plants are edible and which are poisonous. During the earlier time I'm talking about, it was all trial and error! The consequences of an error by the designated camp cook had a direct effect on how long folks survived in a somewhat inhospitable environment.

Until man learned how to build a fire, a hot meal was a rare occurrence. These first campers had to locate something to eat and then find an old snag smoldering from a recent lightning strike. Once they could build a campfire, all they needed then was a supply of wood and grub. History books tell a story about the 'Cradle of Civilization' but they fail to mention early man rocking that cradle by firelight. Our society as we know it springs from those first gatherings. The exchange of information around the campfire led to progress. Each bit of new knowledge that was passed on in such a manner increased their ability to survive!

Except for rare situations, camping today isn't a matter of subsistence. Rather, we head for wild places to recharge our batteries and step out of the concrete jungle for a breath of fresh air! Regardless of the outdoor activity we pursue such as hiking, fishing, bird watching, white water boating, etc., the day ends around a campfire. Sure, in some cases the campfire is inside a modern self-contained recreational vehicle, but nonetheless, day's end finds everyone gathered around a 'campfire'! Once dinner is done, talk turns to the day's activities, and from there to campfires past.

Writing this second 'Outdoor Cookbook' would have been much simpler by compiling recipes and adding a couple of pages on how to cook with a Dutch oven. But, there is much more to camping than just eating good grub at the end of the day! By sharing stories and the experiences of my friends and me, hopefully when you finish reading the book it will have served two purposes. First, everyone in camp will head for bed with a full stomach, and secondly the stories will bring back memories of a past camp with old friends and family and leave the reader with a smiling face! Both telling and listening to campfire stories completes any camping experience for me! So if you've read this far you now know why there are stories in addition to recipes.

For those readers who may not have my first book, *Cee Dub's Dutch Oven & Other Camp Cookin'*, I've included abbreviated sections on the history, selection, and care of Dutch ovens, and how to get started if you're a beginning camp cook.

Tony Kavalok & CeeDub packing out of Gospel Hump
K. Kavalok Photo

═══ HISTORY, CARE, and SELECTION ═══

What we refer to as Dutch ovens, or the camp oven as some folks prefer to call them, arrived in America during the Colonial period. A brand new Dutch straight from the foundry has changed little from those used by the founding fathers! Their use by settlers during the westward expansion is well documented. Not only did they constitute the cornerstone of the early American kitchen they were a valued trade item with Native Americans. It's a little known fact outside the Native American community, but Dutch ovens and other cookware obtained by the tribes after the arrival of European man started a cooking revolution! If this idea seems a little far fetched, go through your camp kitchen and eliminate any pot or pan made of metal as well as everything else you consider essential that Native Americans did not have! Sure we could all probably get by for a weekend camping trip roasting wieners on a stick, but remember these folks camped year round! A Nez Perce friend told me that of all the things obtained through trade with white men, only firearms were more important to her people than iron cookware.

My paper back dictionary defines 'Dutch oven' as "a heavy pot with an arched lid, for pot roasts, etc." We can further expand this definition by adding that it's made of cast iron and less frequently of cast aluminum. It also has three legs approximately two inches in height and a flange on the lid to hold hot coals. The different sizes of DO's are designated by capacity in quarts or diameter. I prefer the diameter designation and the recipes in my book reflect this.

As our society matured, and I say that with tongue in cheek, the use of Dutch ovens and other cast iron cookware declined. Ever ready to hang our hats on something new, we rushed out to buy the latest nonstick cookware spawned by the technological revolution. Then of course came the 'next generation' of nonstick cookware! With each 'improved coating' the manufacturers and marketers threw in a multi-year guarantee telling consumers how many years they would enjoy pans that wouldn't stick. In retrospect it appears to me their marketing techniques were a helluva lot slicker than the coating on their pans! Anyway…in recent years we've experienced a trend of 'back to basics' and fortunately cast iron cookware and "Dutch Oven Cookin'" came into vogue again!

During the 'Nonstick Dark Ages' there were folks who refused to apostatize and didn't succumb to the fervor of the TV pitchmen. DO's and cast iron skillets seemed relegated to outfitter camps, line shacks, and sheep camps as well as the kitchens of those too poor to afford one more modern miracle! These folks kept alive and preserved 'camp cookin'! As the technological revolution accelerated, the already hectic pace of our lives increased as well. Society, like anything else, seeks release under increased pressure. This release came in the form of renewed interest in outdoor recreation.

Back when Dutch ovens and cast iron skillets ruled the culinary world, white water boating remained the province of explorers and frontier dwellers. Major John Wesley Powell planted seeds when he set off in boats to explore the Grand Canyon of the Colorado in 1869 that eventually bloomed into an adventure sport of worldwide proportions! The early entrepreneurs in the outfitting profession who started city folks looking to western rivers for recreation were among those who'd kept Dutch oven cooking alive. I don't have any fancy statistics or graphics to prove this, but the popularity of DO cooking closely parallels the growth of white water boating. The spin-off effect of this jumpstart has led to a tremendous surge in popularity for the venerable old Dutch. Some would call this next remark self-serving, but I believe the world is a little better off with more and more folks discovering the joy of Dutch oven cookin'!

DO's NEED LOVE, TOO!

Whether you buy a new DO or find a used one at a yard sale, it just makes good sense to take care of it! With normal care a Dutch will last a lifetime. In reality they will last several lifetimes, but I for one am not going to worry about what cooking gear I'll need once I leave this life. Speaking of that event, most folks I know would prefer to inherit cash. My old pard 'Catfish,' aka Tom Beck, once said there is nothing easier to move than cash! At this point I don't know how much cash I'll be leaving my son, Brian, but he will for sure need a truck to move the cast-iron portion of his inheritance! Anyway…enough said for the longevity of Dutch ovens!

When you purchase a brand new Dutch, read and follow the manufacturer's directions regarding care and maintenance. They have way more experience than I do, but if perchance you lost the product information, here is the procedure recommended by Lodge Manufacturing. A DO comes from the foundry with a preservative coating that prevents rusting. Unprotected, a new Dutch will rust just from humidity in the air. Begin by washing the DO and the lid in hot soapy water. Rinse it well and when it's completely dry you're ready to start 'seasoning' your DO. You will also hear this referred to as 'curing' but the terms are interchangeable. The folks at Lodge recommend you use vegetable oil or olive oil and not animal fat such as lard. With a paper towel or a new sponge wipe every surface of both the oven and the lid inside and out with a thin film of oil. Put the DO and lid in your oven upside down and place a sheet of aluminum foil underneath to catch any excess oil which may drop off. Close the oven door and set the temperature for 350 degrees and find something else to do for at least an hour. Turn the oven off and let the DO cool down to room temperature in the oven (another 1-2 hours).

The DO is now ready to use. Some folks have been led to believe it requires some mystical miracle voodoo to properly season a DO, but I assure you it's as easy as I've described. But…read on to learn what NOT to do when seasoning a new Dutch!

A buddy of mine who shall remain anonymous operates under the philosophy that 'if a lot does a good job, more will do it better.' It might work in some situations perhaps but not for the job at hand. This fellow admits he did read the directions then decided a thick application of shortening at a much higher heat would produce better results in the same amount of time. Wrong! Increasing the amount of shortening to which you're applying more BTU's than recommended will exponentially increase the potential for disaster! Twenty-one years as a game warden taught me that it's human nature to rationalize one's mistakes and make giant leaps of logic in order to place the blame on someone else. The victim to this leap of logic was present in the house but she happened to be asleep when the 'accident' occurred. A downfall of living in a small rural community is the volunteer fireman could easily be a friend or relative who is very likely to tell all his friends and relatives about the 'stupid' things seen while being a volunteer fireperson. But, I'm getting ahead of myself here.

'TWAS THE WEEK BEFORE ELK SEASON

'Twas the week before elk season and all through the house,
Just one creature was stirring and it wasn't a mouse.
While Mom and the kids slept like the dead,
Dad poured another beer and admired its head.
Knives to be sharpened and saddles to mend,
If left in the house would push Mom 'round the bend.
With the house so quiet 'twas easy to work,
No one to nag or give his chain a jerk.
Before heading to camp his new Dutch must be cured,
His wife he told, "No mess I'll make, I give you my word"!
Like mustard on a wiener the shortening he spread,
He put the Dutch in the oven and carried the rest to the shed.
Chores all done (he thought), upstairs he went,
He shuttered the windows and even the vent.
He crawled in with Mom and was soon fast asleep,

A couple hours passed before the smoke alarm started to **BEEP!**
Fog in their brains they wondered, "What is that clatter?"
Then Mom screamed, **"Fire!"** That's what's the matter!
Visions of embers hastened their nocturnal retreat,
The fire department arrived but had no fire to beat.
Windows and doors they opened to help clear the smoke,
Mom wasn't impressed when Dad tried to joke.
They coiled their hoses and drove off out of sight,
Then Mom and Dad, they started to fight.

The giant leap of logic I spoke of earlier went like this. It was the wife's fault because she gave him the DO for Father's Day and should have foreseen his unfortunate and regrettable lapse of consciousness. I've tried similar logic myself, and I'm here to tell you it doesn't work!

Butch & Pen rafting on Main Salmon
Penny Welch Photo

Matt and Brian go for a "swim" in Ruby Rapids Summer 1997
Penny Welch Photo

BUYING A DUTCH OVEN

Given the choice I prefer to buy products made in America! This includes, of course, Dutch ovens. In recent years I've seen DO's of foreign manufacture appear on the shelves which like most imports have a cheaper price tag. Though I'm just a camp cook and not a trained metallurgist, the difference in quality is apparent. A friend of mine said he'd found a couple worth having after sorting through quite a few. This tells me two things. One, the overall quality is not as good as those produced domestically; and two, the quality control process leaves something to be desired.

This past year my wife and I were treated to a tour of the Lodge foundry in South Pittsburg, Tennessee. On one line we saw DO's manufactured utilizing the same methods used when the foundry opened, and on an adjacent line DO's were being cast using the latest computer controlled technology. As we walked through the plant our guide would point out different individuals and tell us with pride how long a particular person had worked there and in some cases a person who represented a second or third generation family member to work at Lodge! In the quality control lab we saw Lodge products as well as the imports being subjected to the same tests. The pride and craftsmanship we saw at the foundry are mirrored in Lodge's entire product line!

My preference for cast iron dates back many years but aluminum DO's have a niche in my camp kitchen as well. A 12" aluminum DO weighs approximately seven pounds whereas a cast iron 12" DO weighs 19-20 pounds. The lighter aluminum DO's are easier to handle for young kids who don't have the upper body strength of an adult. The weight savings are also a definite factor in my decision to use aluminum Dutch's for white water rafting and horse packing. Besides being lighter, aluminum DO's don't require seasoning and can be washed with soap and water. But, because the iron DO's weigh more they retain heat longer and will reach the higher temperatures necessary to brown when baking biscuits on a cool breezy day. So, there are pro's and con's for each. If you're considering buying a Dutch, analyze your outdoor cooking needs and purchase the type and size of DO which best suits your requirements.

CLEANING AND STORING DO's

Like sourdough starter, the more you use a DO the better it gets. After it's seasoned the first time it will be a color between that of a new Dutch and the shiny black patina of one that's been used for years. The only time I ever use soap on a DO is when it comes out of the box it was shipped in from the foundry. Hot water and a nonabrasive kitchen scrubber will take care of cleaning chores after that. Soaking with hot water for a few minutes will loosen most food residue. Remove all food particles and rinse well with more hot water. When it's completely dry wipe a thin film of oil or grease inside and out just as when you seasoned it initially. Don't neglect the lid either. Condensation collects on the underside and will rust if left on. Before you know it, folks will be asking you how old your Dutch is because of its classic black patina.

Store your DO in a cool dry location. In areas where the relative humidity is high, it's even more important to make sure you wipe the DO down with oil after each use before storing it. Don't overdo the grease as it will turn rancid and a varnish-like residue results which will release itself into the next food you cook. I like to fold up 2-3 paper towels in the DO to absorb any moisture. Also you can take a 4" square of aluminum foil and fold it to the size of an stick of gum that's been folded in half to place between the lid and the Dutch. This allows air circulation and aids in rust prevention.

DUTCH OVEN EQUIPMENT

For those contemplating making the switch from wieners-on-a-stick type camp cooking to Dutch oven cookin' the basic investment to get started will not require a visit to your banker. Once you acquire a Dutch it doesn't take much else to start creating your own menus, however, a few items are mighty useful and will make the tasks much easier.

Probably the most important accessory for the beginning cook is a lid lifter. The lid for a 12" cast iron DO weighs between six and seven pounds. With 18-20 charcoal briquettes on top, it's more than is smart to pick up with a regular kitchen hot pad! After trying several different lid lifters I've settled on the Mair™ Dutch Oven Lifter. Most lid lifters use a hook to pickup the lid and a brace of some sort to keep the lid from tilting and spilling ash into the Dutch. The Mair™ ™ lifter uses a clamp arrangement to stabilize the lid and give more control. On my larger 14, 15, and 16 inch diameter ovens, it really makes moving lids and dumping ash a lot easier and safer.

If you can find them a pair of 'hot pot pliers' will save scorching your knuckles. The jaws on these pliers are offset from the handles which allow the cook to take the lid off a DO to check on progress without subjecting knuckles to direct heat from briquettes on the lid. The hot pot pliers I have also have a small hook that can be used to hook the hot bail of a Dutch and carry it like a bucket.

I also recommend a pair of heavy leather gloves. Try getting a pair at a welding supply store. They are heavy enough to quickly grab a hot coal or briquette that's fallen out of the firepan and toss it back in. When moving hot and heavy objects like DO's they will save you or your helper a trip to the ER. I also keep handy a pair of metal kitchen tongs to pick up errant coals and to arrange coals in the firepan and on my DO's.

As with any endeavor the more one 'gets into it' the more one can spend on accessories and gadgets. The bottom line, though, is a meal will taste the same with these few basics as one prepared by an 'expert'! (Personally, I don't really care for the term 'expert' which I once heard defined as follows: An 'ex' is a has-been and a 'spurt' is a drip under pressure!)

Words of Wisdom

Especially during the dog days of summer set coolers with frozen and fresh produce in the shade. Keep them shut tight. I strap mine shut with cam lock straps to get a tighter seal between the lid and the cooler. Only open them when necessary. To help keep things cold try an old sheepherders trick. Get a couple of old burlap bags at the feed store, soak them with water and drape them over the coolers. The evaporation will keep things cooler than the ambient air temperature.

COOKING TECHNIQUES

Some folks consider camp cookin' an art form of sorts. Most good cooks enjoy the creative process whether a dish is simple or elaborate. There is no denying art plays a part in the creation of a tasty dish that is pleasant to look at as well. The flip side of the creative coin centers on applying just the right amount of heat for the proper length of time. The most expensive ingredients exquisitely prepared will burn just as quickly as a can of store bought beef stew if the cook overloads the DO or gets distracted. With heat adjustments just a twist of the dial away, the stories of food burned at home would fill a small library, I'm sure. Now, take that number and multiply it by the number of variables the camp cook deals with, and you can easily visualize the 'burning potential'! As do most camp cooks, I use various propane or liquid-fueled camp stoves on occasion, but for the purpose of this discussion I'll talk about using charcoal briquettes and/or coals from a campfire for Dutch oven cooking.

Most folks of my generation first recall seeing their folks use charcoal to grill steaks and burgers in the back yard as an alternative to building a campfire. As time passed charcoal began to give way before progress in the form of 'gas grills.' Touted as less messy and more convenient these technological marvels got more people cooking outdoors. Now it seems some folks consider the gas grill part of their camp kit. In recent years I've noticed more and more folks headed to the woods for the weekend with their gas grill lashed down in the bed of the truck. I enjoy grilling stuff both at home and in camp, but I missed the gas grill train and use traditional methods in both locations.

I base my choice of charcoal for both DO cooking and grilling on two factors. First, here in the Intermountain West we have few hardwoods available, and because of that fact most campfires are fueled with coniferous woods, i.e. pine, fir, and/or spruce. The coals produced by these soft woods are adequate for cooking, but they don't get as hot nor do they last very long. Consequently, these two variables alone present problems to even experienced camp cooks. Like everything else in life we have choices and selecting charcoal is no exception. The Constitution tells us all men are created equal but I'm here to tell you all charcoal is not! There may be some regional brands out there I haven't tried, but I've found one national brand to be head and shoulders above the rest. Kingsford Brand® is all I use and Mr. Kingsford is not paying me to say so! Just like the big city chef, the camp cook needs a consistent steady source of heat and Kingsford Charcoal® is always consistent. With these preliminaries and explanations out of the way, let's start cooking.

Before we light our charcoal, though, it's best to figure out first where we're going to cook. Most of my cooking is done on commercially built firepans. These firepans were designed for use on western rivers where regulations prohibit fires built in 'traditional' rock fire rings. There are lots of alternatives to the commercial firepan available to the beginning DO cook. If you can find one, a metal garbage can lid works great. If it has an integral handle, set it up on 3-4 bricks. Also I've seen cooks who used hubcaps with a little sand in the bottom or a wheelbarrow with a layer of sand. In addition there are commercially built cooking tables with optional or detachable windbreaks available. I like the cooking tables and the type firepan I use because of their height. They save a lot of bending over.

Whereas the kitchen cook merely twists a dial to obtain the desired heat, a recipe calls for the camp cook to first figure out how many briquettes needed and then light them ahead of time. Your briquettes will be ready in 20-30 minutes. If it's windy at all, the briquettes will light faster but by the same token you'll have less usable cooking time. (More of those ugly variables the kitchen cook doesn't have to deal with!) In my experience good charcoal will give about 1-1 ½ hours cooking time on a summer day with no wind. Most dishes will cook with one load of charcoal, but the wise cook will start extra charcoal to have on hand if the wind is blowing and for dishes which take longer. Keep in mind it will take several minutes for the Dutch to warm up enough to begin cooking. Time your recipes from when things begin to cook, not from when you place the DO in the firepan, allowing 5-10 minutes time for the Dutch to heat.

FRYING

Just like at home you turn the burner on and adjust it to the desired temperature. In camp place some briquettes in your firepan and set the DO on top. I arrange my briquettes in a circular or checkerboard pattern to evenly distribute the heat. Using a 12" DO, 8-10 fresh briquettes should be sufficient. Of course you can add a few briquettes if you want to brown something quickly and subtract a few to lightly sauté.

BOILING

The same technique is used as in frying. To start something boiling quickly, start with 15-20 briquettes underneath your Dutch. Once it starts boiling remove 5-10 of the briquettes with your metal tongs to gently simmer.

BAKING

Baking requires heat both underneath and on top of the Dutch. Much has been written on the subject of, "How Many Briquettes Do I Use?" Many cooks use what I call the 'rule of two' or the 'rule of three' to calculate how many briquettes to use. It works like this. Take the diameter of the oven and subtract two for the number of briquettes to use underneath and add two to the diameter for the number of briquettes to place on top. The 'rule of three' works the same way. But, I do things a little differently. I'm not saying these two methods don't work, but what I'm saying is I do what works best for me. For instance, if I'm baking a batch of biscuits in a 12" DO, I find 4-5 fresh briquettes will provide all the heat I need underneath. For the lid I place approximately 18-20 briquettes around the outside edge of the Dutch and including a couple in the middle near the handle. With all other factors being equal, this combination will bake biscuits or cornbread in 20-25 minutes. My guess is that the oven is at 350-375 degrees. Part way through the baking process, I will lift the DO up and give it a quarter turn. This helps to evenly brown the bottom of the biscuits. Do what works best for you. It could be a combination will work best. It's just that I've found that using the rule of two or three gives me too much heat on the bottom, and a burned biscuit is more likely to result!

BRAISING/ROASTING

Braising in the oven utilizes a covered dish with a cooking liquid. Of course the liquid forms steam which helps cook the dish along with the heat from the oven itself. A moist cooking method if you wish. An engineer once told me a cast iron Dutch cooks with about 2-3 pounds of steam pressure due to the weight of the lid. If this is in fact true, it lends credence to what DO cooks already knew. A tough cut of meat cooked in a DO is tenderer than if done in a conventional oven. For braising and/or roasting I will use 10-12 briquettes underneath the Dutch and an equal number on the lid. If it's cool or windy, I may increase this by 2-3.

Rather than bore the reader with minutia and expound on all the vagaries of cooking with charcoal outdoors, I leave it to you to experiment on your own. Take what I've written here and use it as a starting point. Some authors I've read consider their formulas 'Gospel' and fervently believe their method is 'the one and only'! So be it, but to paraphrase an old cliché, "There is more than one way to load a Dutch!"

=Applying Heat to your Dutch Oven=

Firepan, camp shovel, metal tongs and charcoal in a chimney starter.

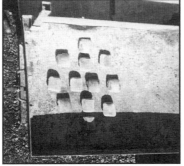

Twelve briquets underneath-plus or minus a couple for boiling and frying

A stack of DO's already cooking and five briquets underneath ready for baking

A 12" loaded with 22-24 for baking

Two 12" DO's braising with 12 briquets underneath and 12 briquets on top. Leg stand allows use of legless 10" aluminum DO at top of stack.

Two 12" DO's cooking with lid stand to stack a 10" aluminum DO without legs

Arrange your briquets like this to keep things warm till serving time

Chamois knows leftovers are on their way

BUDGETS FOR CAMP COOKS

I suspect if you're reading this you have a personal budget. However, if you have so much money you don't worry about such trivial things, it's my guess you normally purchase books, which cost a lot more than this one did! Let's face it we all have to worry how much things cost. How many people do you know would still go camping if they could afford to get on a wide body jumbo jet and fly to some tropical paradise without mosquitoes, chiggers, ticks, etc! Some I'm sure but I'd expect campgrounds to be less crowded just the same!

As with any other endeavor money plays a part. How well we eat when we leave home and head for the woods is not a matter of quantity vs. quality nor is it a matter of good grub vs. barely palatable meals! I believe the investment of some time spent planning and by using common sense, camp cooks can serve delicious and nutritious meals on a reasonable budget. The biggest budgetary trap I see is the dependence on 'convenience' type food items. Notice I said 'dependence and not 'use'! If you looked in my camp kitchen would you see items that fall into the 'convenience' category? Yes! But as someone far wiser than me once said; "Moderation in all things!" So how do you cut you grub budget and still keep folks coming back for seconds? Read on! I'm sure you can come up with some of your own cost cutting ideas!

BE HAPPY

If you wish to be happy for one hour
.... get intoxicated
If you wish to be happy for three days
.... get married
If you wish to be happy for eight days
.... kill your pig and eat it
If you wish to be happy every day
.... learn to fish

-Ancient Chinese Proverb

$ TIPS $

When you shop look for bargains and don't buy something just because it looks good and is ready to eat! If you're buying bacon for instance, buy the 'ends & pieces' package which should save you about a buck a pound.

Instead of several cases of soda for the kids, mix up powdered soft drinks and freeze them in reusable containers. You save money over the pop and this cuts how much you'll spend for ice.

Make a batch of stew or chili and freeze ahead of time rather than spend money on canned store bought items. The more you take from home the less you'll spend at the store. This goes for desserts, etc., as well as for main entrée's.

If there are things you seem to go through at a fast pace buy them in bulk if possible.

Plan your menus. Don't just head for the market and buy until your coolers are full.

Take advantage of your leftovers. Let the kids have them for between meals snacks or to tide them over until dinner is ready.

For extended trips plan to use fresh meat and produce early. Check the dumpsters at a campground sometime to see how many of these items get trashed cause the cook tried to stretch their use over the whole trip.

──────── **Words of Wisdom** ────────

If kids are in camp try to set aside one cooler for their use. When they come charging into camp looking for a snack or a cool drink they won't upset the cook by pawing through every cooler before finding what they want.

──────────────────

COMMON SENSE and CARDS

"That will never happen to me!" How many times in life do we say this to ourselves! Whether a fleeting thought or an actual verbalization, human nature kicks in when we see a news report about someone lost in the woods. The more time a person has spent beyond roads end, the more likely the thought crosses the mind of "How could anyone be that dumb!?" Yet year after year we read in the paper of folks who are overdue and the local search and rescue unit gets called out. Often the subject of the search is not some 'Pilgrim' on a maiden hike into the wilderness, but someone the reporter describes as knowledgeable and woods-wise. The majority of time the lost soul ends up walking out or is located in good condition by the searchers. We all like happy endings, but unfortunately some searches result in calls going out to contact the next of kin and the coroner.

Over the years I've been called to assist with several search and rescue efforts. The time of year, weather, age, and condition of the subject, plus a host of other variables come into play as to how long someone can last in the woods. More often than not the actions of the lost person will determine how long it takes searchers to find that person! Maybe it's human nature, but it seems that once a person realizes he's lost, he feels compelled to walk. Because he starts walking and keeps walking in the wrong direction, searchers end up looking in the wrong places. It boils down to…a moving target is harder to hit!

Prior to hand held Global Positioning System (GPS) receivers becoming widely available, a map and compass were the best insurance someone heading into the woods could take. It doesn't matter whether you're hiking up a creek for an afternoon's fishing or headed into a wilderness area for an extended stay, the potential for getting lost always exists!

When we head for the woods there are all sorts of emergency items one can carry, but two major ones stand out in my mind. The first and most important being "Common Sense"; and, secondly throw in a deck of playing cards!

I taught hunter education for twenty-one years. When students were told of those two items, without exception everyone in a class would get a puzzled look and ask, "Why?" when I made this suggestion. The cards go hand in hand with the first, most important thing one can carry in the woods, the "Common Sense." When a person first realizes he is indeed lost, the most important thing he can do is STOP! Once a person gets as comfortable as possible given the situation he should pull out the deck of cards and begin playing *Solitaire!* Before he knows it, someone will be looking over his shoulder telling him to play the Red Ten on the Black Jack. To some, this may sound facetious, but someone telling me how to play *Solitaire* ain't near as bad as spending time and energy walking in circles waiting to be found!

═══════ Beginning Cook ═══════

In this series of photos my son, Brian, shows just how easy it is to make a dump cake.

Brian arranges six briquets underneath the Dutch

Dump in about 6 cups fresh black berries

Sprinkle ½ cup flour over fresh berries for thickening

Like the recipe says, dump in a cake mix

Like the recipe says, dump in a 20 oz. bottle of Seven-Up®

Dump cake baking with six briquets underneath and 20-22 on top

Where is the ice cream, the dump cake's done!

GARBAGE
DO's and DON'T's

Most authors wouldn't even think of including a section on *garbage* when writing a cookbook but I believe it appropriate in a book for camp cooks! After preparing a meal at home, clean up is a breeze. Wet garbage, i.e. vegetable peelings, etc., go into the disposal or the compost pile, re-cyclables go into the appropriate card board box, and the rest goes into the trash to be placed curbside on garbage day. The camp cook most likely will not have all of these options.

When camping in developed sites with garbage service not much changes from cooking at home but there are still things to consider. During peak use times garbage pickup schedules may be such the cans overflow creating an unsightly and unhealthy situation. So whether camping in a developed site with garbage services or an undeveloped site where 'Pack It In & Pack It Out' regulations apply, keeping trash to a minimum makes life easier for all.

Despite education and enforcement efforts there are those who think littering is acceptable behavior. As a conservation officer my fellow officers and I spent a lot of time enforcing littering laws and educating the camping public. One particular incident comes to mind. One day while on routine patrol I saw an airborne white flash through a screen of trees adjacent to a streamside campsite. As I pulled into the camp a fellow was getting ready to heave a second white garbage bag as far as he could out into the Salmon River. He set the sack down and got a surprised look on his face when I bailed out and quickly opened the tailgate on my truck. Surprise turned to chagrin when one command sent my Black Lab 'Snoose' after the evidence! The lesson this fella learned that day is it's much cheaper to haul it than heave it!

Years ago folks would burn everything they could and bury the rest. Just last week while moose hunting with a friend we camped at a site, which has been used for forty years at the end of an old, two rut road. Walking out in the timber behind camp I found numerous old cans and bottles once buried but now littering the forest floor. My guess is they were originally unearthed by a black bear in search of grub. Almost any wild critter will dig if it smells food and most folks won't be able to dig a hole deep enough to discourage a bear! Garbage gravesites aka backcountry landfills are no longer appropriate or legal.

In my camp I separate garbage into wet and dry items. Any paper products I can burn I will. **Don't** however, throw a wad of wet paper towels and paper plates into the fire and expect them to completely burn. If you can see something won't burn just put it in a sack for transport home. **Don't** throw candy or granola bar wrappers coated with aluminum foil into the fire. Yes, I know a hot enough fire will burn even aluminum beverage cans but after years of digging through other campers' fire pits and packing out partially burned cans and wads of foil, I advise against placing non-organic material in a campfire. **Don't** attempt to burn cantaloupe rinds, potato peelings and the like. **Don't** tempt critters into coming into camp at night or while your out fishing by placing yesterday's garbage behind the tent. **Do** put it in the truck, an empty cooler, which is strapped shut or hang it in a tree. **Do** as much kitchen prep at home ahead of time as possible. Trim or peel vegetables and pack them in re-sealable plastic bags. **Do** reuse these same bags for leftovers or throw away scraps. **Don't** use any more glass containers than absolutely necessary! Re-pack liquid items such as vinegar, whiskey, etc., in plastic containers. **Do** crush metal cans and plastic containers, as they will take up less room. **Don't** forget the micro-trash! Cigarette butts, gum wrappers, and bottle camps though individually small will still aggravate those who use the same site after you! **Do** spend as much time planning on how to deal with camp refuse as you do in planning your menu's! **Do** follow the 'Golden Rule' and leave your campsite as you would expect to find a campsite.

DEDICATIONS

HANK, JACK, and ME

All three of us moved to Challis, Idaho, within a year or so of each other. **Hank Ketchie** worked for the US Forest Service as a forester and arrived in 1977. I moved to Challis as a rookie game warden in November, 1978. Jack, when he did work, worked for me, and moved there in February, 1979. Jack and I had been acquainted for only a short time and didn't know each other very well before we both moved to Challis. I met Hank within the first week or so and it didn't take us long to become friends. During our first conversation we realized we'd attended Utah State University at the same time. Though we hadn't met there, we did have friends in common from college days. Being stationed in a small central Idaho cow town as a resource manager or a game warden presents its own unique social obstacles. We weren't social outcasts but socially we were cast together!

That first fall of '78 went by in a blur. Trying to learn a new patrol area kept me going both night and day. Right after the first of the year the boss called me up and said to get my affairs in order 'cause I'd be spending five weeks at the police academy. Trust me, my social affairs were nonexistent which meant it didn't take me long to get ready and be gone. When I finished up in mid-February, I drove over to Wayan where I'd previously been stationed, before heading home to Challis. Jack had been staying with a friend of mine, Steve Somsen, since I'd left for Challis in November. He wasn't real glad to see me, but with a little persuasion loaded up and headed north with me. The first time I ever saw a horse smile was the next day when I unloaded Jack at my rented pasture in Challis. In Wayan the snow had been up almost to his belly while in Challis bare ground told Jack he'd indeed made a good move!

Besides being a forester, Hank was a horseman. Not a cowboy, but a horseman! He did a little horse trading, horse training, and shod horses to support his hunting and fishing habits. A couple of days after I got back with Jack, Hank came by to see him. Hank didn't look too long before he said, "Besides being ugly, what other bad habits does he have?" I told him of the ones I knew but also said there were probably others yet unknown, which would surface soon enough!

On several occasions I loaned Jack to Hank for various little chores like packing out an elk or two. In addition we made several rides together both for work and pleasure. It didn't take long to compile a pretty long list of Jack's faults. I don't know who had the most to learn, Jack or me! Any question I asked resulted in a common sense answer that came from experience and not from a book or magazine. Besides sharing his knowledge, Hank built a pair of pack boxes for me, doctored my stock when I was out of town, and showed me the lighter side of shoeing horses and mules. Like the time a two-year old filly getting shod for the first time got touchy and began wrestling Hank for control of a front foot. She won the match but when she set it down she ended up with her legs crossed. Hank didn't cuss or get upset, but simply said, "I like a lady who crosses her legs when she gets nervous!"

On the professional level Hank and I worked timber sales together. Hank looked at things from the silvicultural standpoint and I from a wildlife management perspective. On our days off we hunted, fished, and explored the Pahsimeroi Valley, Hank riding Dan or Spot and me on Jack. Whether sitting in a duck blind or the cab of a truck coming back from a horse trip we always found something to talk about. I was the first person who knew that Hank and his wife, Deb, were expecting. Likewise Hank called me first when he killed a bull elk with his bow, or when his dog, Rev, learned a new trick. But, Hank kept a secret from me along with others for nearly three years. He had cancer!

Towards the end, Rich Rodgers, Nick Zufelt, and I traveled to Salt Lake City, Utah, to visit Hank. Hank could still get around a little and after the others said their goodbyes and left, he walked me to the elevator. As the door closed Hank said, "Jack has improved enough I'd put him in my string!" Hank said this with dry eyes, but mine were still running when I hit the ground floor. These many years later, two emotions come to mind when I think of Hank! For the short time we spent together I'll always be grateful, but I'll always be sad because of how short the time ultimately ended up being!

Hank Ketchie - Little Morgan Creek-Custer Co., Idaho
Annie Sennelick Photo Collection

SHOESTRING BULL

The mountain men and free trappers who explored the Intermountain West in the early 1800's referred to it as their "possibles" sack. A small leather poke sack with essentials they might 'possibly' need in the course of their travels. Such items as flint, steel, tinder, whetstone, needle and thread were staples along with other small items each individual deemed essential. Today's equivalent takes the shape of a fanny pack or day pack in which we carry things we might need during our trip outdoors be it a day hike or an extended stay. Today's "possibles" most likely include matches in a waterproof container, a map and compass, an extra shoelace, etc., and other important small items excluding of course cell phones and GPS Receivers!

What's included with one's "possibles" varies according to a person's wants and needs. Sometime when you're out in the woods with a bunch of folks, sit down after dinner and have everyone go through their "possibles" to see the variety of things that folks consider essential. For sure there will be things peculiar to each individual and include items which at first glance appear insignificant! But...there are those occasions when one of these seemingly insignificant items tucked away in the bottom of a day pack saves the day. Such a day occurred for my pard, **Rich Rodgers**, on a cold, snowy day in mid-November, 1983.

Rich, Tom and Bill Beck, and I were hunting deer and elk out of a horse camp on Indian Creek Airstrip on Middle Fork of Salmon River. A wall tent with smoke wisping from the stack and the glow from a lantern greeted Rich as he trudged in about an hour after dark on the third day. Before he said a word, we knew from the grin on his face and blood on his boots that he'd connected. His first elk, a six-point bull, needed packed out the next day. Starting out as a city kid from Glen Ellyn, Illinois, another dream came true for Rich that cold, snowy November day. Other dreams already realized by Rich included being a collegiate All-American football center at 5' 10" and 210 pounds, obtaining a MS in Range Management on a NCAA scholarship, becoming a farrier under the tutelage of Henry Ketchie, and marrying Sue.

Happy hour that evening extended until way past supper as Rich told and re-told the story with more detail each time. After describing where the bull was down, the trail, and the heavy snow conditions, we decided to walk in leading a packhorse, bone the elk, and backpack the meat up to a ridge top where we could get the packhorse with minimal difficulty. One of the details Rich had added the third or fourth time he told the story concerned the steepness of the hill where the bull lay. He told us he'd tied the bull to a short, scrubby tree to keep it from sliding down into the bottom of Mowitch Creek.

Rich, Tom, my Black Lab, 'Snoose,' and I left camp in the gray light of dawn leading Black Jack, one of my packhorses. Where Rich's tracks from the previous day hit the horse trail I loosened his cinch and tied him securely to a tree about forty feet off the trail. If recollection serves me correctly, we dropped about 500-600 vertical feet through a foot plus of snow on a mountain steeper than a cow's face to get to the bull.

It wasn't the fact that Rich had tied the bull up to keep it on the face of the 'earth' that struck me. It was how he tied it up which caused Tom and I to bust out laughing! The previous day Rich had quickly realized how a precarious position this bull was in if he expected the rest of us to help pack it out. Had the bull slipped into the bottom, it would have been easier to just pack in a frying pan and eat him on the spot! To stabilize the critter, he'd started with a piece of rope from his day pack and tied it to the antlers. This chunk of rope was way too short to reach the only scrubby Doug Fir tenacious enough to grow on such a steep slope. Scrambling up to this scrubby Doug Fir, he tied his remaining piece of rope and stretched it out towards the first line. Guess what? We've all been there! He was still short! Having once been a football player, Rich knew the importance of having an extra shoelace. Connecting the two lengths of rope was a shoelace from among his "possibles"!

Whenever campfire talk turns to elk hunting, this bull will forever be known as the "*Shoestring Bull!*" The last time I saw Rich before he passed away from cancer, the telling of this story again brought the smile from that cold, snowy November night in the wall tent back to his face.

Cee Dub, Rich, Jim Van Ark & Snoose
Rich is holding The Shoestring Bull
C. W. Welch Photo Collection

RELIGIOUS BEDROLL

For two or three years running I was the victim of a conspiracy. No matter how carefully I scheduled things a conflict would arise which precluded my going on Middle Fork of Salmon River float trips with my pards. Instead, my house became the staging area for everyone as they gathered from the four corners of the country. These pre-launch rendezvous left me feeling deflated and left out, like the perennial bridesmaid who never becomes a bride! And much like a wedding, the festivities were great fun but the next morning after everyone departed, a feeling of being unfulfilled would descend. Actually, though, what I really suffered from the morning after might be better described as a hang over. Anyway…

One such rendezvous included **Greg Rost**, aka Rosterman, a friend from college days at Utah State University. Greg graduated a year ahead of me in 1973 and went on to complete a MS Degree in Wildlife Management at Colorado State University. While I worked on a dude ranch, drove long-haul truck, and trapped grizzly bears prior to becoming a game warden, Greg began his career with the Division of Animal Damage Control with the US Department of the Interior. By the time of this reunion, Greg had advanced to an Area Supervisor position in Elko, Nevada. Long into the night, we regaled the group with stories from college days and beyond. Long after the liquor store closed, things started to dry up with many stories yet to tell.

Greg called for an intermission, walked out to the garage, and rummaged through his river bag for his 'river jug'! In he came with a 1/2 gallon of Christian Brothers Brandy®. He was willing to sacrifice some of what he'd brought for riverside campfires for one more round with his pards! I broke the seal and commenced pouring. This particular jug came equipped with one of those new-fangled plastic pouring spouts. Since it seemed to inhibit the flow, I popped it out…the better to quickly pour a man-sized drink!

The next morning while I cooked breakfast, everyone including Greg packed their river bags and got ready to go. Greg came into the kitchen, grabbed his jug and cranked the lid down tight. An ounce of prevention is worth a pound of cure as the old saying goes, so Greg wrapped his jug in his bedroll to guard against accidental breakage.

I later learned that the first evening at Trail Flat Camp, Greg learned something about the bottles that the good Brothers put their brandy in. In order to completely seal the jug, it's imperative to leave the little new-fangled pour spout in the neck of the bottle! With little daylight left to dry his sleeping bag, Greg spent the night rolling around trying to get comfortable with the Christian Brothers! Unsubstantiated reports relayed since that hot sticky night indicate Rosterman indeed prayed for the continued good health of a certain game warden until fitting revenge could be meted out!

Our next rendezvous ended before it began with the crash of Greg's plane. To this day when I pass the crash site I raise my hand and pretend I'm taking a drink from his 'river jug' and say, "Here's to you pard, wherever you are!" Ten years later, I still have more than memories of Greg. Before he moved to Alaska he left a bay horse and his saddle with me for safekeeping. Greg called him Rusty but he's known as Slim in my string. On more than one occasion riding down a trail alone on Slim I've reached into saddlebags for a small flask containing a certain brand of brandy and taken a swig before thanking my old pard for his friendship and the use of his horse!

Greg waiting for the coffee to brew Middle Fork Salmon
Tom Beck Photo

AS CLOSE TO HEAVEN
AS ONE CAN GET

Enroute to becoming employed full-time as a game warden for Idaho Department of Fish & Game, I detoured to the National Park Service for three field seasons. In 1975, '76, and '77, I worked in and around Yellowstone National Park on the Inter-Agency Grizzly Bear Study Team (IGBS). Our summer crew consisted of sixteen people. Some were still in college and others of us had graduated and were seeking any job in our field until we could find permanent employment. **Bill Hoskins** and I made up part of the second group. By the time I met Bill in 1975 he'd already spent several field seasons in Yellowstone on various fisheries projects. A native of Tennessee, Bill found himself pulled West after attending Tennessee Tech.

The college kids would start pulling out by mid-August for school leaving those of us with six-month appointments to finish out the field season. Of the four seasons, fall is my favorite, and for those three years Bill and I partnered up for September and October. Bill owned a little house in Gardiner, Montana, just outside the North Entrance to Yellowstone Park. During the summer we worked ten days on and four days off. In the fall, however, we often worked out of Bill's house and had weekends off. After summering in the back country, Gardiner's limited social life made for a more well-rounded field season.

Before I get to the morning where for a minute we both thought we were in Heaven, I better tell you more about Bill. "Willie," as a few of us called him, made work seem like a pre-paid adventure. A master of understatement, Willie could take any situation and put a humorous spin on it. Like the day we spent trying to radio track one of our bears whose signal indicated it might have met an untimely end. Aerial tracking flights showed the bear hadn't moved in about ten days. As we homed in on the signal we expected to find either that the bear had managed to pull the collar off or find a dead bear. In a small clearing we found the remains of the bear scattered about, obviously scavenged by another bear. After surveying the scene, Willie, in a dry tone of voice said, "I don't think this one is goin' to make it!"

When working with Bill, a person never had to worry about wearing a watch. You could set a clock by Bill's stomach. Years later when I became a parent, I'd think of Willie when my son would wake us up for a feeding every two hours all night long. Bill didn't cry when he wanted food, but he could sure get your attention when it was time to eat!

Anyway...the morning at issue came about in late September after the boss sent Bill and me out to finish up some vegetation analysis plots. One evening we found ourselves pitching camp where the 'Reclamation Road' crosses Snake River just south of Yellowstone National Park. Both the location and weather were exquisite calendar material. The fall colors exemplified why fall is my favorite season! I awoke the next morning in this beautiful place wondering what had brought me back to consciousness. I heard Willie rustle and roll over, but neither of us said a word. As the cobwebs cleared I started to sort out sounds to figure out what had awakened me. I dismissed the bugle of an elk up on the ridge above camp as being too far away to wake me. But when another bull answered from just behind camp, I knew then what had roused me back to the land of the living. Neither of us spoke for fear of breaking the spell. Between bugles a new sound intruded on the stillness of the morning. A flock of geese announced their morning flight down the river with muted honks. As they passed over we could hear the rattle of pinions with each wing beat. The farther bull faintly bugled as the geese passed out of hearing. I broke the silence in the tent by asking a question directed as much to myself as Willie, "Are we in Heaven?" Bill, with his inimitable delivery replied, "I don't think so because I can still smell our socks!" We both agreed Heaven might be an OK place to spend some time if every morning started as ours just had!

Bill ended up running the License Data Base Section for the Montana Department of Fish, Wildlife and Parks. The last time I saw Bill before his passing from a cerebral hemorrhage, we both showed up at a rendezvous of past and present members of the IGBS at Porcupine Guard Station along the Gallatin River in Montana. One evening sitting around a campfire sipping an ice-cold beer, we again relived that magic fall morning on the banks of Snake River! Even today the stench in hunting camp of three-day-old socks will rekindle the memories of spending those three fall seasons with "Willie!"

Bill Hoskins with Bear #8. Flat Mtn. Arm, Yellowstone National Park

C.W. Welch Photo

GAME WARDEN DOG

When I hired on as a conservation officer for Idaho Department of Fish & Game (IDFG) in September of 1978, **Snoose** turned six months old. I'd come by her four months earlier when I ran into a friend at IDFG Headquarters where we both had meetings. Russell had hired on as an officer a couple of years earlier and I still worked as a Wildlife Technician. At a break in the meetings I caught Russ up on what I'd been doing and told him about the awesome log home I had rented near Wayan in SE Idaho. He told me he had the perfect pup to live with me in such a great place. He still had two female pups from a litter of nine who needed homes. Being a canine sexist at the time, I told him 'No Thanks!' No females for me. I'd always had males. Apparently, Russ didn't have any better luck peddling those two pups during the day 'cause when I arrived at the restaurant that evening he bought me a beer, one of many that night, and started his sales pitch again.

After rolling out of bed the next morning I needed three things really bad. First, and most important, a couple of aspirin, followed by a cup of coffee; and, last, a hot shower…in that order. Not being the first guy to wake up with the events of the previous evening being a little fuzzy, I 'thought' I remembered writing Russ a check for $75.00 late the night before. (It was brought to my attention later that I actually wrote the check about closing time.) When I got out of the shower I looked in my checkbook. Sure enough, the self carbon copy of the last check said 'Pay to the Order Of' Russ Kozacek. My consolation being at the time that although Russ did succeed in selling me a dog, I hadn't bought dinner or a beer all night! Anyway…Snoose moved to the big log house in Wayan with me. She spent the summer leaning how to fetch, stay out from underfoot a saddlehorse, and how to load in a pickup truck.

The transformation from civilian to game warden doesn't happen overnight. How successful a game warden is depends on both tangible and intangible criteria. One of the tangible criteria being, of course, the apprehension of violators who go home with pieces of paper labeled 'Defendant's Copy' in their wallets! Six weeks into my career and hunting seasons in full swing, the only citations my name appeared on listed me as 'Assisting Officer.' With elk season a week old my ego and confidence hit rock bottom. Sure, I had encountered some folks with problems, but their stories always seemed truthful to me. So I'd give them a weak verbal warning and go off in search of a 'big game case.' At the time I naively believed everyone always told the truth to the game warden!

On Sunday of the second weekend of elk season, Snoose and I left the house in the gray light of dawn, headed for Jacknife and Tincup Creeks. I started making the rounds of trailheads and campgrounds thinking that if things didn't change, I would find myself back driving a truck. About noon I checked a camp of moose hunters breaking camp after getting a bull packed out. I then headed for McCoy Creek. I hoped that I could find a violation in my neighboring officer's area! By mid-afternoon, and several camps later, my luck hadn't changed. Discouraged doesn't even come close to how I felt. I stopped at a creek thinking Snoose might enjoy a swim, as the day was getting warm. My heart dropped when I got out of the truck! No Snoose! I started backtracking, asking folks I'd just checked if they remembered seeing my dog in the back of the truck. No luck!

I headed back to Tincup Creek, not believing I could have missed her for such a long time. Finally I ended back up in the camp where I'd checked the moose hunters. There she lay contentedly chewing on a leg bone that they'd discarded. Apparently she hadn't missed me at all. After chastising her I loaded her back up and decided to check a couple of camps where no one had been present in the camp on my earlier swing through.

As I pulled into the first one, a fellow came riding in leading a couple of packhorses. He told me he'd killed an elk, and that it was boned out in meat sacks on the pack stock. I felt pretty good writing him a citation for an unattached tag while he unloaded the packhorses. But something still sort of gnawed at my subconscious. Why I felt compelled to go through the meat sacks I'll never know! Unless one has the space to lay out the individual pieces of boned meat to determine their anatomical location you can't make sense of what your looking at. This guy and his buddies had made it easy. When I located a heart in the third sack of meat it didn't raise any alarm. In the fourth sack, though, I found *another* elk heart, which did set off all sorts of warning bells. Then it was obvious! These guys had killed two elk and tried to disguise the fact by boning the meat and mixing it up. I didn't hesitate to give Snoose the credit for leading me to that breakthrough big game case.

I spent two thirds of my career with Snoose! Over the years she assisted me on several cases and on occasion made cases outright for me. Snoose didn't spend much time at home those first ten years. Most of the time she rode in the back of the truck, but fixed-wing aircraft, helicopters, drift boats, and rafts suited her just fine. Except for being in a duck blind, she was happiest trailing along ahead of my saddle horse as I pulled a pack string  somewhere in the back country! The day finally arrived when it got too difficult for her to jump up into a pickup truck.

Snoose spent seven years in retirement before she passed on just a couple days short of her fourteenth birthday. I still consider that $75.00 the best money I ever spent. A couple of years ago I returned the favor to Russ when I sold him a female pup out of my Chesapeake, Sis! Russ just wrote a check and saved me the expense of buying him dinner and beer for an evening!

Black Jack & Snoose, Wayan, Idaho, Summer 1978
C. W. Welch Photo

APPETIZERS

Camp "Horse Ovaries"

The hunters coming out of the elements like to unwind and snack while the camp cook finishes his chores and starts dinner. The following were served at our deer camp in 1997, and are great dishes to bring along and have handy to tide the appetites over.

Ingredients:

Pickled okra
Smoked Salmon
Cheese and crackers
Dill pickles, homemade
Pistachios
Chips and salsa

Chile 'n' Cheese Spirals

Ingredients:

8 oz. cream cheese, softened
1 cup (4 oz.) shredded cheddar cheese
½ cup (4 oz. can) diced green chiles
½ cup (about 3) sliced green onions
½ cup chopped red bell pepper
½ cup (2 ¼ oz. can) chopped ripe olives
4-6 (8") soft taco-size flour tortillas
Salsa, on the side

Combine cream cheese, cheddar cheese, chiles, green onions, red pepper, and olives in a medium-size bowl. Spread ½ cup mixture over each tortilla, then roll up. Wrap each roll in plastic wrap and refrigerate for 1 hour. Remove plastic wrap and slice each roll into six ¾ inch pieces. Serve with salsa for dipping.

This treat is a family favorite for river trips, parties, or at home. It's great as an hors d'oeuvre or to tide the kids over before supper. Finely dice some jalapenos to give it some zip.

Dick's Hot Mustard

Ingredients:

1 1/3 cups (4 oz. can) dry mustard
   (Colman's, if available)
2 Tbsp. sugar
2 tsp. salt
¼ cup oil
½ cup wine vinegar

Combine all ingredients, blending well. Refrigerate.

Dick Kirtner
Little Cabin, Bartlett-Hopkins Ranch
South Fork of Clearwater River

Dick Kirtner, our friend and neighbor, brought this by one night to go with some corned venison and sesame seeds. My stepson, Matt Dykas, and a friend of his from Michigan, Chad Vliek, were visiting during hunting season. Chad took a pretty good-sized dip of the mustard. As the tears were streaming down his face, he asked, "What in this mustard makes it so hot?" Matt calmly answered, with a little grin on his face, "That would be the mustard!" So, if you enjoy hot mustard, you'll enjoy this one. A little bit goes a long way.

Corned Venison 'n' Seeds

Ingredients:

1/2-3/4 lb. corned venison, pre-cooked and cooled,
   sliced in pieces about the size of crackers
1/2 cup sesame seeds, toasted if available
2 Tbsp. Dick's Hot Mustard

We use corned venison as a variation of the Oriental hors d'oeuvre of pork 'n' seeds. If you don't have corned venison, you can substitute pastrami. Gather round the table with a cold beer or your favorite beverage and enjoy this tasty treat.

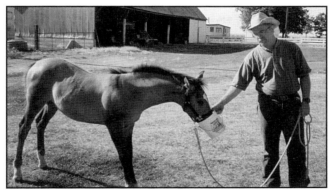
CeeDub serves Buckshot a beer Summer 1998

Penny Welch Photo

Nachos

Ingredients:

Tortilla corn chips
Meat, if desired, such as shredded pork, or beef prepared
  Mexican style
Tomatoes, chopped
Onions, chopped
Cheese, grated
Olives, chopped
Sliced jalapeno peppers
Other toppings as desired
Sour cream, salsa, and/or guacamole

Place the largest foil plate you can find that will fit in the bottom of a 16" Dutch oven. Put a layer of tortilla chips on the tin plate. Add the meat and other garnishments putting the cheese on top. Place the lid on the Dutch and heat for about 15 minutes or until the cheese melts. Use about 20-25 briquets on top of the Dutch oven to quickly heat the nachos. Slide tin plate of nachos from the Dutch oven. Serve with sides of sour cream, salsa, and/or guacamole as an added treat. Preheat the oven while you build the nachos if you're in a hurry. Kids enjoy creating their own version of this snack. Have fun with this one and add any of your favorite ingredients which I may have left out.

—— Quick Dutch Oven Pizza ——

Ingredients:

> 1 12-14 inch pizza crust *
> 1 14 inch foil or aluminum pizza pan
> 1 small jar, or homemade, pizza sauce
> 1 package sliced pepperoni, or other desired meat
>   topping
> Olives, diced
> Tomatoes, diced or sliced
> Onions, diced
> Green peppers, diced
> 1/2 cup grated mozzarella cheese
> 1/2 cup grated cheddar cheese
> 1/4 cup Parmesan cheese
> Other toppings, as desired

*There are several options in choosing your pizza crust. The choice may depend on how much time you have. The simplest one is to buy a ready-made crust in the store, whether completely baked or one that is partially baked. Using one that is already pre-baked will cut down on the baking time for the pizza. Another option for the crust is to use a packaged mix and make according to the instructions. Also available are crusts in the dairy section of the grocery store. Just open the can and roll out the crust. However with this method, you will need to transform the pizza crust from a rectangle shape to a circular shape, but this can be done easily.

Coat the pizza pan with a thin layer of vegetable oil to prevent sticking no matter which type of crust you choose. Put the oiled pan in a 16" Dutch oven. Place the crust in the pizza pan. Smear the pizza sauce over the crust to within one-half inch of the edges. Arrange the pepperoni or meat topping evenly on top of the sauce. Distribute the other condiments over the pizza. Sprinkle the mozzarella and cheddar cheese over the toppings and sprinkle the Parmesan cheese on top. You may choose to add the toppings in another order. There is no wrong way to do this, only lots of right ways. Put the lid on the Dutch oven, and place over 4-5 briquets in the firepan. Place 18-20 briquets on the lid. If using a pre-baked crust, bake for about 15 minutes or until heated thoroughly and the cheese melts. If baking entirely, bake for 20-25 minutes. Remove from heat and take off the lid. Slide the pizza pan from the Dutch oven, cut, and serve.

──────────── **Words of Wisdom**────────────

If you're camping in an undeveloped site become familiar with minimum impact camping techniques.

────── Seafood Lasagna Rollups ──────

Ingredients:

> 6 lasagna noodles
> 1 15 oz. can Italian tomato sauce
> ¼ cup grated Parmesan cheese, as garnishment

Filling:

> 1 pkg. crab flakes or chunks
> 1 cup cottage cheese, drained
> ¼ cup grated Parmesan cheese
> 1 egg
> 1 Tbsp dried parsley flakes
> 1/8 tsp. onion powder
> 1/8 tsp. garlic powder

Cook noodles according to package directions. Rinse in cold water, and drain. Combine the filling ingredients with a fork. Spread 1/3 cup filling, or about 1/6 of the mixture, on each noodle and roll tightly. Spread 1/3 of the tomato sauce on the bottom of a 10" Dutch oven. Place the rollups seam-side down on the sauce in the Dutch oven. Pour remaining sauce over the rollups. Bake covered for about 30 minutes using 4 briquets under the Dutch oven and 10-12 briquets on the lid. Garnish with additional grated Parmesan cheese.

A LASTING GIFT

As a kid my only concern with Dad's camp kitchen had to do with when dinner would be served. Upon receiving my driver's license as a teenager, I started going on trips with my friends. Without parental guidance and the absence of anyone remotely close to being a camp cook, our chow fell into the 'Very Basic' category! After just a couple of these trips I asked Dad if I could borrow his camp kitchen. Without going into details Dad based his decision in part on my track record of borrowing tools, pocketknives and gas money. Mom came to my rescue. She started culling some of her kitchen stuff and picked up new stuff for the house. With this modest start my camp kitchen came into being.

A few years later an academic miracle occurred! I graduated from college. (My philosophy of, "To hell with excellence, mediocrity will suffice," contributed to my taking six years to get a four year degree.) In recognition of this miracle Mom and Dad gave me a graduation gift I use to this day! After years of camping in an old army surplus squad tent, they'd bought a new cabover camper. Mom outfitted the kitchen with new pots, pans, and utensils. The old squad tent and their cast iron cookware now became 'parental surplus' and my camp kitchen took a quantum leap forward.

The Dutch oven and the skillets given to me twenty-five years ago remain the core of my camp kitchen. Two or three of the pieces they gave me date from just after WWII when they were married! Over time I've accumulated another 25+ Dutch ovens, several more skillets, and four cast iron griddles. Properly cared for, cast iron cook gear will last longer than the cook!

———————— Words of Wisdom ————————

Give your wooden cutting boards and utensils a coat of mineral oil on occasion. It will improve their appearance and they will last longer.

LAS PIEDRAS

For those of you who didn't take high school Spanish this translates to 'The Rocks'. *Las Piedras Ranch* owned by Dwain and Sandy Riney of Montgomery, Texas, is aptly named. Located in Real County, WNW of San Antonio, *Las Piedras Ranch* exemplifies the Texas 'Hill Country'! Their ranch, though not large by Texas standards, supports a healthy population of native wildlife and is also host to numerous exotic species. These wild, free ranging exotics escaped from neighboring ranches years ago. Dwain and Sandy recently invited me down to cook for some of their hunters. This particular hunt is a 'special hunt' for both the Riney family and the hunters. Once a year Dwain and Sandy donate a hunt for exotic species at *Las Piedras* to the Montgomery County Cattle Barons' Ball and benefit auction. The money raised from this annual event benefits the Montgomery County Unit of the American Cancer Society.

In the course of my visit Dwain pulled out the 'ranch recipe box' and selected several favorites of his and Sandy's that he thought I'd like. In addition Sandy has since called me with a couple of other old family favorites. We hate to think of family heirlooms disappearing, but it happens when you prepare these recipes. My thanks to Dwain and Sandy for sharing them and inviting me down to share their corner of heaven in the Texas Hill Country!

Frank Riney & Bart Cobb await CeeDub's dinner at *Las Piedras*
Dwain Riney Photo

Texas Caviar

The first time my wife and I tasted this dish, we had stopped at *Venison World* in Eden, Texas, to see if they would carry my cookbook. After visiting with Maggie for a while we struck a deal. She would carry the book in her store if I would try a sample of Texas specialty foods. The 'Texas Caviar' caught my eye so we packed a couple jars of it all the way home to Idaho. My intention at the time was to come up with my own recipe via 'reverse engineering.' However, fate intervened and Sandy Riney of *Las Piedras Ranch* shared her mother's recipe with me. Sandy serves her 'caviar' atop miniature corn muffins as an hors d'oeuvre. I find it also goes well as a dip or served on crackers. If you get through Texas, try the store bought variety and if you're at home make your own with Sandy's recipe.

Ingredients:

2 cans of black-eyed peas, drained
1 cup salad oil
¼ cup red wine vinegar
½ cup thinly sliced onion
(use small boiling-type onions, if available)
½ tsp. salt
2 cloves garlic (use whole ones and remove after marinating; or for more garlic taste,
finely mince and leave them in.)
cracked pepper to taste

Mix all ingredients well and pour into a jar. Let marinate for two weeks before serving. Sandy said it's OK after a day or two, but the only way she can get it to last for two weeks is to make it the day before she leaves on vacation. The first time I made this I started with 1 lb. of dried black-eyed peas. I cooked them according to the package directions and doubled the rest of the ingredients.

Sandy Riney
Las Piedras Ranch
Real County, Texas

JERKY and SMOKED FISH

Drying meat began with pre-historic man and remains today as one of the easiest methods of preserving meat and fish. Though not recorded by these early campers, someone figured out when campfire smoke drifted past a drying rack, the smoke itself imparted a different flavor to the finished product. With a little more experimentation they figured out smoke from a fire fed with pine left a taste modern man would identify as tasting like turpentine, while fruit wood and some hardwoods yielded a much more pleasing flavor.

The biggest difference between the 'Original Recipe' and what we buy in the store or make ourselves is salt. In those early days salt was not available except in coastal areas or where salt deposits existed. The term jerky and the use of salt in its preparation are relatively new on the scene. *Journal of a Trapper* by Osborne Russell and edited by Aubrey L. Haines, depicts the life of a mountain man 1834-1843. Russell makes numerous references to 'dried meat' but does not mention using salt as part of the process. The term 'jerky' is most likely derived from the Spanish term *charqui* that refers to thin strips of dried meat, the Spanish version of 'Original Recipe'!

I've never tried to dry meat or fish without first soaking it in brine or using a dry rub, but I have sampled air-dried fish. A. K. Scott, a Fisheries Enforcement Officer for the Nez Perce Tribe, shared with me one evening chinook salmon prepared in the traditional way. This fish was not smoked nor brined. A. K. merely hung the fillets in a screened box until they reached the desired dryness. I seldom use the term delicate, but no other word adequately describes the taste.

I've tried many recipes for both smoked fish and jerky over the years. Many of these turned out too salty for my taste. As a result when I try a new recipe I make a small batch first just to see how salty it ends up. The recipes here agree with my family's tolerance for salt and taste great to boot!

We make our jerky from deer or elk, but beef can be substituted. I suggest getting an 'inside top round' from your local butcher. It will weigh about eight pounds or so.

This cut is free of connective tissue and fat. Trim other cuts well. I like my jerky fairly thick, so I slice mine across the grain from a quarter to one half inch thick. If you like it thinner, put the meat in the freezer until it's almost frozen before slicing for ease of cutting. Depending on thickness and desired dryness, it will take approximatly 3 pounds of meat to yield 1 pound of jerky. Experiment for the best results.

As for the smoking part, I suggest new comers use one of the commercial 'Smokers' and follow the manufacturer's directions. Also, there many homemade smokers in use ranging from old refrigerators to old metal drums. Basically, though, all smokers use the same principal. They all have wire racks placed over a heat source. The smoke comes from wood chips or shavings that smolder to produce the smoke. Food dehydrators now on the market can also be used to make jerky. With this method, the spices and seasonings used in a brine or rub flavor the jerky. Liquid smoke in the brine will give a more authentic flavor.

However...whether you use a smoker or a dehydrator use extra care in preparing your jerky. Research indicates food born bacteria such as E. coli can withstand temperatures in excess of 150 degrees Fahrenheit. If your smoker has a thermometer, be sure the air temperature inside the smoker exceeds 200 degrees for at least 10-15 minutes. If using a dehydrator, consider making up a little extra brine and storing it in a separate container. Just before you're ready to put the meat in the dehydrator bring this extra brine to a boil and dip the meat in it for a couple minutes. Add any dry seasonings such as pepper afterwards.

You can make jerky out of just about any type of meat you want, the two exceptions being bear and mountain lion. Both these critters are known to carry trichinae. As with pork, it takes a temperature in excess of 170 degrees to kill trichinae. Few, if any, smokers will reach temperatures high enough to eliminate this pest. Some folks just up the river from where I live learned this lesson the hard way a few years ago when they ate jerky made from a mountain lion.

As with anything else you choose to take on, do some homework before you get started for enjoyable results.

"THE" Jerky Recipe

Brine:

¼ cup non-iodized salt
2/3 cup sugar
2/3 cup brown sugar
1 ½ cups soy sauce
3 cups water
1/8 cup Worcestershire sauce
5 cloves garlic, chopped
    or, bulk, chopped garlic in a jar
1 tsp. black pepper
1 Tbsp. dried onions
2 Tbsp. pepper sauce
½ Tbsp. Tabasco®
    (more, if you are brave)
1 tsp. liquid smoke

Mix the above ingredients in a plastic, glass, or crock container, using hot water to help dissolve the salt and sugars.

The above will typically handle about 8-10 pounds of meat. I have tried this on elk, deer, and lean beef with great success. Trim off all fat and connective tissue. Nothing will sour a jerky connoisseur more than a fine piece of jerky ruined by a glob of smoked fat! I like to slice mine fairly thin to aid in drying time. This is best done when still slightly frozen. Add sliced meat to mixed brine and make sure all meat is submerged. I use the old Cee Dub "plate as weight" method as well. I like to keep the meat in the brine for at least 12 hours. One can leave it in for several days if making large batches with limited drying space. Stir the mixture on occasion. If you are using the brine again soon, the left over brine can be drained and used one more time.

After the brining is complete, remove strips from brine, rinse in cool water, drain, and place on smoking/drying racks.

Allow the meat to air dry for one hour. This is an important step! A "glossy look" will form when dry (the "pellicle"), and this aids in preservation. The final preparation separates the "men from the boys": *real* men (women, too) add liberal amounts of ground pepper to the meat at this point (prior to smoking)…and, those not so daring will go on to the final step!

If using a commercial smoker, smoke for 1-3 hours with your choice of fuel and then complete the drying time. Or, use an oven, dehydrator, etc. Times and dryness of finished product will depend on drying method and personal preference!

Jeff Heindel
Idaho Fish & Game
Eagle, Idaho

—————— Smoked Salmon ——————

Marinate salmon for 5-6 hours in Teriyaki Marinade. Pat dry. Smoke over apple or pear wood very slowly, for about 4 hours. This is my favorite marinade recipe to use.

Basco's Teriyaki Marinade

Ingredients:

1 12 oz. bottle of soy sauce
½ cup brown sugar
1 cup water
6 cloves garlic, minced fine
2 Tbsp. finely minced fresh ginger

Place all ingredients in a sauce pan and bring to a boil. Allow to simmer for 5-10 minutes. Cool and store in refrigerator. Marinate any red meat or chicken for 1-2 hours prior to cooking.

Dave McGonigal
Idaho Fish & Game
Boise, Idaho

Strawberry Oat Bars

Ingredients:

2 ¼ cups flour
1 ¾ cups brown sugar
¾ tsp. soda
¾ tsp. salt
1 ½ tsp. cinnamon
1 ½ cups butter, softened (no substitute)
3 ½ cups regular oats (1/2 cup reserved)
2 tsp. vanilla
Strawberry jam, seedless

Combine flour, sugar, soda, salt, and cinnamon. Cut in butter. Stir in oats and vanilla. Press one half the mixture into greased 13" x 9" pan or a 12" Dutch oven. Spread jam on the matter in the pan or Dutch oven. Add the reserved one half cup oats to remaining batter in the bowl and mix. Crumble the rest of the mixture over the jam. Bake in the oven at 375 degrees, or place in Dutch oven over 4-6 briquets with 18-22 briquets on the lid. Bake for 25-30 minutes.

Sue Kinner
Grangeville, Idaho

Put a couple of these in your day pack before you leave camp.

Words of Wisdom

No matter how good the weather has been, it can turn bad quickly. I cut an old pair of hip boots off just below the knee. When things get wet and muddy in camp I use them for camp slippers of sort. Dry footwear is a must!

If you leave camp to hike or fish for the afternoon, lock your valuables up in a vehicle. Two legged wild animals may come into camp and help themselves.

MODERN DAY PILGRIMS

Look up "Pilgrim" in the dictionary and you'll find the following definition: "(1) a wanderer, (2) one who travels to a shrine or holy place as a religious act, (3) any of the band of English Puritans who founded Plymouth Colony in 1620." As often occurs, a word or term falls through the proverbial crack and takes on an entirely different meaning.

Somewhere along the way though, and it was way before my time, "Pilgrim" became synonymous with such terms as rookie, tinhorn, greenhorn, etc. To one degree or another each of us falls into this category at times. For example, in my own case if you were to plop me down in the middle of a major metro area I'd stick out like a porcupine at a cat show! On the other hand…I've observed dwellers of suburbia and other city folks venture to roads end and beyond wandering aimlessly in the forest. It's been fun, educational, and a study in man's ingenuity!

EXAMPLES

I'm a firm believer in going prepared but be realistic when you pack. I've seen it with boaters, horse packers, backpackers and day hikers. No matter what you do, you can't stuff ten pounds of potatoes into a two-pound sack! There **is** a difference between essentials, necessities, and luxury!

Take a few minutes to plan your camp. Don't, for example, pitch your tent made of synthetics down wind of the campfire! Speaking of tents, dome tents should be staked and weighted down. It doesn't take much wind to displace them and given ideal terrain they will roll like a tumbleweed and just as far! I'll leave potential destinations to your imagination.

If your outdoor recreation includes boats or pack stock, take the time to learn some basic knots. Properly tied up they'll still be there in the morning when you wake up. I've never met a sailor or cowboy who prefers to be afoot.

Besides, the cure for injured pride still eludes medical researchers!

Put the rain fly on the tent when you pitch it. Don't wait for the rain to start! And, before you go to bed make sure your firewood pile is covered and the toilet paper is in a WATER PROOF BAG!

Make sure anything which uses fuel of any kind is well maintained and in good operating condition. Turn off and double check connections on gas stoves, lanterns, and heaters. The best-case scenario might be you're out of gas in the morning. On the other hand only size differentiates a house fire from a tent fire, and asphyxiation is still asphyxiation!

If you're car camping, make sure you turn the ignition off as well as accessories like dome and cargo lights, or your stay may be much longer than planned. Vehicle emergency brakes are primarily designed to prevent FORWARD motion. If launching a boat or parking on a steep slope, chock the wheels for peace of mind!

Wild animals are just like college kids. Free food is the best! Take to heart campground notices advising of their presence. The size of the critter is of little importance. You'll be just as hungry if a bear cleans out your cooler, as you'll be if mice or chipmunks try samples of everything within reach!

Of course I could go on but by now you should have my point. In my own study of "Pilgrims," I've determined it takes three things to climb the ladder and be rid of the label "Pilgrim." As with any endeavor, first one needs knowledge to advance beyond the basics. Secondly, is the ability to apply one's knowledge to any given situation and not repeat mistakes, even those made by others! Of the three, tunnel vision presents the greatest obstacle for most folks, myself included.

As someone once said, "Don't sweat the small stuff!" If you do commit a faux pas, don't make the same mistake twice, grin and bear your companions' ribbing. And above all, remember you're having fun!

BREADS

PITCH IN and PITCH OUT

Two things act as magnets on little boys, mud puddles and pitch. I'm not talking about the card game "Pitch," but sap from coniferous trees. When the folks took us kids camping, despite repeated warnings and dire threats by Mother, I usually managed to get the sticky stuff on my hands, clothes, and in my hair within thirty minutes of getting to camp. I did it to my folks and my son did it to me. As an old cowboy buddy of mine told me when my boy was born, "You don't pay for your raising till you raise one of your own!" That particular saying has proven true on many other occasions! Anyway...

Like many situations in life there is 'the easy way' and 'the hard way' to remedy the situation. Normally the first line of defense in most situations requiring cleanup is soap and water. Besides being sticky in the first degree, pitch immediately attracts **dirt**. Pitch on a kid's hands will just smear and spread with soap and water. Anything the kid touches ends up sticky, which if he handles enough stuff will wear the pitch off his hands! That is an option, but one most mothers would rather not exercise. Unless you take a set of full body restraints to camp, don't even think you can successfully comb a wad of pitch out of your kid's hair!

For a quick fix, dig around in your camp box for your charcoal starter fluid. Any other petroleum distillate, such as white gas, kerosene, etc.; will dissolve pitch, but charcoal lighter seems to be the least harsh. Just squirt a little bit in your hands and rub the spot, then wash with soap and water. To clean clothes, first change into something clean and soak the spot with the lighter fluid and work it into the fabric. Repeat a couple of times then hang on a limb to dry. Getting the stuff out of one's hair is a little more difficult. Soak a washrag and gently massage the pitch to dissolve and repeat if needed. Soak another washrag with warm water and rinse. Of course, I shouldn't have to say this, but if it's after dark, use a flashlight or other source of light, not firelight or gas lantern!

Dave's French Toast

Ingredients:

1 loaf French bread, sliced
3-4 eggs
4 cups of milk
1 tsp. vanilla
1 Tbsp. cinnamon
1 tsp. nutmeg
4 cups corn flakes, crushed
Syrup, or other favorite topping

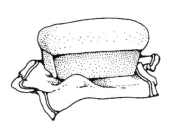

Put the corn flakes in a self-sealing container and crush with a rolling pin. This can also be done on a sheet of waxed paper or aluminum foil. Place the crushed corn flakes in a bowl for dipping. Crack the eggs into a separate large bowl. Add the milk, vanilla, and spices. Dip the bread into the milk mixture to coat the bread. Then roll the bread into the corn flakes. Fry the French toast on a griddle until golden brown on both sides. Serve with butter, syrup or your favorite topping.

Dave McGonigal
Boise, Idaho

Beer Bread

Ingredients:

3 cups self-rising flour
2 tsp. sugar
1 - 12 oz can or bottle of beer at room temperature

Mix preceding 3 ingredients. Grease and place in Dutch oven. Bake for approximately 50 minutes or until done using 4-5 briquets on bottom and 25 briquets on top, or in oven for 50 minutes at 375 degrees.

This quick bread recipe helps round out a meal of stew or soup. If you plan on this for a meal, be sure to hide a can of beer beforehand if you're getting low.

Dumplings

Ingredients:

1 1/2 cups flour
1 1/2 tsp. baking powder
1/2 tsp. salt
1 egg, well beaten
1/2 cup milk
Large kettle of boiling water

Beat egg, add milk, salt, flour, and baking powder, working into smooth dough. If dough is sticky, add a little more flour. Knead well. Divide dough into about 6 small pieces. Make a smooth dumpling by working or shaping the dough into round balls in your hands. Drop dumplings in boiling water and boil for 10 minutes. You can take one out and cut open to see if they are done.

When cooked, take out into a bowl and cut them in halves, using a string to cut the dumplings (makes them more even or smoother) or using 2 forks, tear dumplings in two. Do not cook them too long or they will get soggy. The dumplings must be cut into halves immediately. Cook a few at a time. Do not crowd them. Do not cover while cooking. Once they start cooking, turn heat down to medium and cook slowly, but keep water boiling.

Jeanette Krupicka
Wilber, Nebraska

I learned how to make "real Czech dumplings" like these from my wife's aunt, Jeanette, during our visit with Jeanette and her husband Kenny in 1999.

Words of Wisdom

When pitching camp always look around for dead trees and those with a noticeable lean. Set your tent up well away from projected impact points should a windstorm come up over night.

73

Mexican Corn Bread

Ingredients:

1 cup flour
1 cup yellow corn meal
1 Tbsp. baking powder
1/2 tsp. salt
1 egg
1 cup buttermilk (or milk)
1/3 cup olive or vegetable oil
1 Tbsp. Mexican seasoning
1 4 oz. can diced chiles, if desired

Mix the wet and dry ingredients separately then pour wet ingredients into the dry ones. Stir until well mixed then pour into a well greased 10" Dutch. Bake for 20-25 minutes with three briquets underneath and 14-16 on top. Make sure you lift and turn the Dutch a partial turn every 8-10 minutes so the bottom browns evenly. Serves 4-6.

In the alternative, a shortcut method for cornbread can be to use two 8 1/2 ounce packages of corn muffin mix and follow the directions on the box for preparation, adding herbs or other seasonings to the batter. Bake in a 12" Dutch oven according to the instructions above. Serves 6-8.

Focaccia Bread

Ingredients:

4 large pieces Focaccia bread
1/2 stick butter

Put bread in a 14" Dutch oven. Melt butter separately, and pour over bread pieces. Warm for a few minutes in the Dutch oven until hot.

Often when heading to camp, I will stop at a bakery and pick up different breads that just need to be warmed up. Focaccia bread adds a special touch if you're planning on Italian cuisine.

Garlic Bread

Ingredients:

French or Sheepherder Bread
1 cube of butter
5-6 cloves garlic, minced
Grated cheese
Italian herbs

Melt the butter in a small container. Add the minced garlic. Ladle the butter and garlic over the bread that has been cut and placed to fit in a Dutch oven. Sprinkle cheese and herbs onto the buttered bread. Place the lid on the DO. Load the top of the lid with about 20-25 briquets to toast and brown the bread.

Garlic Bread

Ingredients:

French or Sheepherder Bread
1 cube of butter
5-6 cloves garlic, minced
Fresh basil, chopped

Melt the butter in small container. Add the minced garlic and basil. Drizzle butter, garlic, and basil over the bread that has been cut and placed to fit in a Dutch oven. Place the lid on the DO. Load the top of the lid with 20-25 briquets to warm or toast and brown the bread, butter, garlic and basil.

These are just a couple of the many variations on an age-old favorite. Garlic bread is quick, easy, and goes with most main dishes or can be served as a snack. It's always a crowd pleaser.

Hush Puppies

Mix together the following dry ingredients:

1 ½ cups white corn meal
¼ cup sifted all-purpose flour
2 tsp. baking powder
1 tsp. sugar
1 tsp. salt

Stir the following three ingredients together and add to dry ingredients:

3 Tbsp. grated onion, or finely diced green onions
1 beaten egg
¾ cup milk or buttermilk

Mix well and drop by the spoonful into hot, deep fat. Turn once and/or cook until puppy floats.

Sandy Riney
Las Piedras Ranch
Real County, Texas

Butch in a "bread making" mood
Penny Welch Photo

Irish Soda Bread

Preheat a 12" Dutch oven by putting 20-25 briquets on the lid and the loaded lid placed on a lid stand for about 10 minutes. This equates to preheating the oven to 375 degrees. Stir together in a large bowl:

> 2 cups sifted all-purpose flour
> 3/4 tsp. baking soda
> 1/2 tsp. salt
> 1 Tbsp. sugar

Cut into the flour mixture with a pastry blender, until the consistency of course corn meal, the following:

> 6 Tbsp. chilled shortening

Stir in:

> 1/2 to 1 cup raisins, optional
> 1 tbsp caraway seeds

Add gradually:

> 1/2-2/3 cup buttermilk at room temperature

The mixture should not be dry. Knead briefly and shape into a round loaf or a 9"x5" one. Put the dough in the greased Dutch oven, or a bread pan if using conventional oven. Cut a bold cross on top, letting it go over the sides so the bread will not crack in baking. Brush top with milk. Bake for 40-50 minutes. To test for doneness, notice if the loaf has shrunk from the sides of the pan.

Serve this with corned beef and cabbage to complete a 'real' Irish supper.

Words of Wisdom

Dish soap, hand soap, and the like should be stored separate from food items to protect against accidental spills. It doesn't take much liquid dish soap to ruin everything in a cooler or food box.

Quick and Easy Bread

Ingredients:

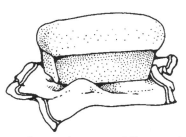

2 ½ cups warm water
2 pkgs. dry yeast
4 Tbsp. shortening
4 tsp. salt
4 Tbsp. sugar
6 cups flour

Dissolve yeast in water. Sift flour, salt, and sugar. Mix yeast mixture, shortening, and half of flour mixture for 2 minutes. Blend in remaining flour mixture. Grease sides of bowl, place dough in bowl, cover, and let rise near heat for 30 minutes. Remove from bowl and onto floured surface. Knead a few times and place in greased pan. Cover and let rise for 40 minutes or ¼" from top. Bake 40 minutes at 375 degrees. Remove and brush with butter.

Mike McLain
Colorado Division of Wildlife

Spider Bread

Ingredients:

1 cup cornmeal
1 cup all-purpose flour
1 tsp. baking soda
½ tsp. salt
¼ cup granulated sugar
1 cup buttermilk
1 egg, beaten
2 Tbsp. butter or margarine, melted

In a large mixing bowl, blend all the dry ingredients. Add buttermilk, egg, and melted butter. Lightly blend until just mixed. Pour into well-greased 10" Dutch oven using 4-6 briquets under the Dutch oven and 18-20 briquets on the lid to bake, or 9" or 10" cast iron frying pan and bake. If no cast iron frying pan is available, use a large cake pan. Bake for approximately 25 minutes at 350 degrees. Spider bread is done when toothpick inserted into bread comes out clean.

—Wheat-Free Cornbread or Muffins—

Ingredients:

2 cups cornmeal
2 eggs, beaten
2 cups buttermilk
1 tsp. salt
2 tsp. baking powder
1 tsp. baking soda
2 Tbsp. vegetable oil

Mix together eggs, buttermilk, and vegetable oil in a medium-size mixing bowl. In a separate bowl, combine dry ingredients and stir into egg mixture. Pour into 12" Dutch oven; or, a well-greased 9" baking pan or 12 muffin cups. Place the Dutch oven in the firepan with 5-6 briquets under the Dutch oven and 20-25 briquets on the lid; or, bake in the oven at 425 degrees. Bake for 30-35 minutes or until done. For sweeter cornbread, add 2-3 tablespoons sugar.

Our friend, Sandy Rost, developed a wheat allergy several years ago. Since then we've looked for recipes that do not use wheat for use when Sandy is in camp. If you're the camp cook, it doesn't hurt to ask folks ahead of time about food allergies. It's much easier to plan ahead than scramble to find alternatives when you are already in camp.

———— Words of Wisdom ————

If your pets go to camp with you keep them under control just as you'd do at home. Other campers won't appreciate them running around. Whether in the suburbs or the great outdoors, an obnoxious barking dog is still an obnoxious barking dog. Also most states have regulations concerning dogs at large harassing wildlife.

BREAKFAST

MAKING DO

Every camper ends up in camp minus from one to any number of necessities. The name of the game then becomes do without or make do with a substitute. When one forgets the can opener, for example, an old pocketknife can be sacrificed and other than being a pain in the butt for the cook, camp life goes on. On occasion I or someone in camp has carved a stirring spoon from a scrap of wood or made a DO lid lifter from a green tree limb. Of course the more complicated the item, the more ingenuity required.

In 1983 another conservation officer and I spent a couple of weeks re-doing the flood irrigation system at a IDF&G back country ranch. I didn't miss the metal spatula that first evening when I grilled pork chops, but it was noticeably absent the next morning when I went to mix up some 'Poor Man's Sourdough Pancakes.' I've yet to see the pancake which one can flip with a fork! That morning we settled for granola bars and coffee but it was obvious we needed something to flip pancakes and turn eggs.

That afternoon Terry Williams and I set out to solve the problem. Terry started out by taking the metal lid from a coffee can and gently hammering it as flat as possible on the chopping block. First he would hammer one side then turn it over and hammer the other side. Within 10-15 minutes it looked like a round piece of sheet metal. Meantime I cut a straight section of a mountain mahogany tree about 10" long and an inch in diameter. With the saw blade on my sheath knife I cut a groove in one end approx. 1 1/2" deep. Then taking a leather punch I bored two holes about a half-inch apart through the portion of the limb with the groove.

Using two old pieces of strap iron and a pair of vice grips, Terry bent one side of the lid up so it would fit into the groove on the handle. We set the turned up edge of the lid into the groove and punched two holes with a horseshoe nail. Two minutes and two small pieces of baling wire later, we had a serviceable metal spatula. It wasn't 'purty' but it served our purposes. So next time you're in camp and realize you've left something at home, look through your miscellaneous and see if you can come up with a substitute!

Baked Oatmeal

Ingredients:

2 eggs
1 cup sugar
½ cup vegetable oil
3 cups quick oatmeal
1 cup milk
1 tsp. baking powder
Brown sugar
Dried or fresh fruits, nuts

Mix eggs, sugar, and oil in bowl. Add oatmeal, milk, and baking powder. Pour mixture into 12" Dutch oven and top with brown sugar. Dried fruit, fresh fruit, and nuts may be added. Fresh fruit should be added during the last 5 minutes of cooking. Bake with 4-6 briquets under the oven and 18-22 briquets on the lid, or bake in the oven for approximately 50-60 minutes at 350 degrees.

Dutch Babies

Ingredients:

3 eggs, well beaten
½ cup sifted flour
½ tsp. salt
½ cup milk
2 Tbsp. cold butter
Powdered sugar
Lemon juice

Blend the eggs, flour and salt. Add the milk. Spread side and bottom of iron skillet with cold butter. Pour batter into the skillet. Bake uncovered at 425-450 degrees until lightly brown. To serve, dust with powdered sugar and lemon juice.

Sandy Riney
Las Piedras Ranch
Real County, Texas

—— Bacon and Onion Potatoes ——

Ingredients:

1 lb. bacon, cut into small pieces
2 onions, diced
4-6 cloves garlic, minced
2-3 lbs. potatoes, sliced
Seasonings to taste
1 lb. cheddar cheese, grated

Brown bacon and onions in a Dutch oven. Drain off some of the bacon grease. Add garlic, and stir in potatoes. Cover, and continue cooking for 30-40 minutes or until potatoes are tender using 5-6 briquets under the Dutch and 14-16 on the lid. Add the cheese, melt, and serve. Serves 8-12.

—— Easy Dutch Oven Breakfast ——

Ingredients:

½ lb. bacon, cut up
1 medium onion, chopped
1 32 oz. bag frozen hash browns
1 doz. eggs
1–1 ½ lb. cheddar cheese, grated
1 8 oz. jar salsa, if desired

Preheat 12" Dutch oven over 10 briquets. In the heated Dutch oven, brown the bacon, adding the onion, and cook until clear. Remove the bacon and onions, draining on paper towels. Wipe excess grease out of Dutch oven and then put Dutch oven back over hot briquets. Fry potatoes until golden, then mix the bacon and onions back into the potatoes. Break the eggs into a medium mixing bowl and beat. Pour over the potato mixture. Cover with preheated lid and cook until eggs are almost solid, about 25-35 minutes. Sprinkle with grated cheese and continue cooking until eggs are set and cheese melts. Just before serving, top with the salsa, if you wish. Use about 18-20 briquets for the lid.

When not working for our printer, Joslyn & Morris, Inc., Bob Stauts spends much of his free time hunting, fishing, and rafting in the desert country of SW Idaho and adjoining areas of Nevada, Oregon, and Washington. He has also become a Dutch oven cooking enthusiast. You only have to read Bob's recipes to see that Bob likes his grub 'hot & spicy'! Bob's recipes typify those of many camp cooks. At the end of a long, hard day the cook creates an awesome meal out of what's in the grub box and the day's bag.

Eggs "Fizz"irenctum

This recipe comes from a Winnemucca Basque gentleman during a snowy September bow hunt. The desired effect from breakfast was accomplished. (Heats you up and keeps you regular!)

Ingredients:

1 doz. eggs
6 English muffins
1 large can of stewed tomatoes
6-8 jalapeno peppers
1 small can green chiles
3 cloves garlic

Saute garlic and jalapeno peppers in olive oil. Add tomatoes and green chiles. Bring to a boil, then poach all the eggs by spreading evenly throughout the surface of the pan. When the eggs are done, serve on fire-toasted (if available) English muffins. Serves 6.

Robert Stauts
Boise, Idaho

Elk Sausage Scramble

Ingredients:

2 lbs. sausage, elk or venison
2 Tbsp. olive oil
1 doz. eggs
Seasonings, if desired
1 cup grated cheese
Salsa, if desired
1 pkg. tortillas

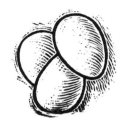

Fry the sausage in the olive oil. Drain off any excess grease. Break all the eggs into the sausage, add seasonings, and stir until done. Top with the grated cheese and let it sit for a couple of minutes to melt the cheese. Top with salsa, if desired. Serve with warmed tortillas.

Words of Wisdom

Keep a small bottle of chlorine bleach in your camp kitchen. Take a couple of quarts of water and add a teaspoon of bleach. Use this solution to wipe off your cutting boards and prep areas.

Rib Stickin' Breakfast

Ingredients:

3 lbs. sausage
20 slices of bread, crust removed
12-18 eggs, beaten
1 lb. cheddar cheese, sliced
Seasonings to taste

Cook the sausage in a Dutch oven, drain, and set aside. Break the bread into small pieces and place in the bottom of a Dutch oven. Pour the beaten eggs over the bread. Place sliced cheese and sausage in layers over the mixture. Add seasonings. Cover and cook for approximately 30 minutes using 4-6 briquets under the Dutch and 14-16 briquets on the lid. Check to see when the eggs are done. Serves 10-16.

Sunday Morning Quiche

Crust Ingredients:

6 oz. cream cheese
1 cup butter
2 cups flour
(or, use a ready-to-bake pie crust)

Filling Ingredients:

4 eggs
2 cups whipping cream
¾ tsp. salt
¼ tsp. pepper
1/8 tsp. ground red pepper
1/8 tsp. nutmeg
Chopped cooked bacon, ham, etc.
1 ½ cups Swiss cheese, grated
1/3 cup green onion tops, chopped
2 Tbsp. flour

Other possible ingredients might be chopped morel or other mushrooms, crab, shrimp, sun dried tomatoes, fresh spinach.

Combine crust ingredients, working into a ball. Roll out and place crust in a pie pan. Bake at 400-425 degrees for 10-15 minutes. If using a Dutch oven, place pie pan on a rack in a 12" Dutch oven. Place Dutch in firepan with about 10 briquets under the Dutch and cover with preheated lid using 20-22 briquets, and bake for 10-15 minutes. Cool the lightly precooked crust and brush with melted butter or olive oil. Combine other ingredients for filling and pour into crust. Continue to bake at 300-325 degrees for approximately 30 minutes or until knife poked into filling comes out clean, using 8-10 under the Dutch oven and 18-20 briquets on the lid. Let stand 15 minutes to cool.

Dave McGonigal
Boise, Idaho

The first time Dave made this for us, he debunked the myth, "Real Men Don't Eat Quiche!" Not only do "real men" EAT quiche, they can MAKE them, too!

CAMP CREATIONS

Few things in life end up being written in stone, the exception of course, a few short words on a gravestone that marks a final resting place. I've run across cooks who treat every recipe card as a piece of granite. Changing a recipe crosses their mind just before they consider voluntary commitment to an institution! In an extreme case, a cook I know totally changed his menu one night for the lack of a certain spice! Camp cooks rarely have that luxury. My personal opinion is, if someone is that hidebound they should cook for survival purposes only and take up something like underwater basket weaving when they want to have fun!

If you truly enjoy camp cooking, an empty Dutch oven should be to you what an empty canvas is to an artist. The artist begins with daubs of paint on a palette while the camp cook opens the grub box and takes stock. Regardless of the colors used or the contents of the chuck box, only imagination and creativity limit the final product. The end result should be pleasing for both artist and cook. The difference being the painting ends up gracing a wall and the meal graces a table.

Many recipes in this book and those still in my files got their start in camp. Hunting season ends up being a month long carousel of company and camps. Everyone shows up with plenty of grub. For convenience, we'll prepare some main dishes at home then take them to camp frozen. These are great when everyone gets in late. Also we have plenty of basics such as spuds, onions, dried beans, rice, and baking supplies. For the first few days if you were to sit back and silently observe, you'd think we actually had a plan. The last few days things change. Mealtime finds the cook rummaging through the grub box and coolers scratching his head trying to figure out just what to fix. Leftovers might show up as a side dish or the cornerstone of something new. The resulting meals end up being equal parts availability and necessity. Whether you're cooking for a crew in camp or the family on the patio, fill your Dutch with creativity and everyone will be back for seconds!

— Chilly Morning Chili Cheese Pie —

Ingredients:

3 4 oz. cans chopped green chiles, drained
4 cups (1 lb.) shredded cheddar cheese
1 cup (1 envelope) dried milk
3 cups water
1 ½ cups buttermilk baking mix or Bisquick®
6 eggs
1 lb. bacon or sausage, fried and crumbled
1 medium onion (optional) sauteed in fat or raw,
    chopped
or raw, chopped1/2 tsp. oregano (optional)
1/2 tsp. basil (optional)
1 tsp. Worchestershire sauce (optional)
    (Rather than using oregano, basil, and
    Worchestershire sauce;use cumin and chili powder)

Spray a 10" Dutch oven with a non-stick spray, or coat with oil. Sprinkle chiles and cheese evenly in the oven. Beat eggs, water, dried milk, and Bisquick® together until smooth. Mix in the crumbled bacon and any optionals you choose. Pour this mix into the Dutch oven. Bake about 40-45 minutes or until a knife blade comes out clean. Use about 6 briquets under the Dutch and 10 on the lid. Serves 6.

Mike McLain - Middle Fork of Salmon River, 1992

—————— Hearty Hash Browns ——————

Ingredients:

6 leftover baked potatoes, cubed
½ cup olive oil, or vegetable oil
5 cloves garlic, sliced or minced
1 medium onion, chopped
¼ green pepper, chopped

Heat olive oil in 12 or 14 inch Dutch oven. Add garlic to oil and cook until tender. Add vegetables and ham. Cook until heated thoroughly and flavors are blended.

Baked Omelet

I start this dish on my camp stove and finish with charcoal, but it can be done entirely with charcoal. If you're not using a stove, start with 10-12 briquets underneath a 12" Dutch oven and have an additional 20 ready for the lid.

Ingredients:

6 eggs
½ cup milk
½ cup crumbled bacon (substitute chopped ham or
   brown some sausage and crumble)
8 oz. grated cheese, your choice
½ cup diced tomatoes
½ cup diced onions
½ cup diced green or red bell pepper
1 cup sliced mushrooms, fresh if available
jalapenos, if desired, to add some fire

Beat the eggs and milk well with a wire whisk and season to taste, if desired. Pour eggs into Dutch oven which is hot enough to start cooking. Caution – don't get your Dutch oven too hot or you'll scorch the eggs.

Sprinkle remaining ingredients, except the cheese, over the eggs. If you start on the stove, set the Dutch in your firepan with 10 briquets spaced underneath and put the lid on with about 20 briquets on top. Bake for about 10 minutes. Sprinkle cheese on and set the lid back on until the cheese melts.

Chili Hash

For a quick breakfast or lunch, add chili with beans to left over hash browns. Heat and sprinkle with grated cheese. Serve with or in tortillas with some salsa.

Dan's Breakfast Chicken
—————— and Eggs for One ——————

Ingredients:

1 ruffed grouse (or remains after someone uses
    #00 buck shot instead of bird shot)
2 Tbsp. olive oil
½ cup beer
1 spoonful canned chiles
1-2 eggs

Brown the "chicken" in a small amount of olive oil in a Dutch oven or skillet. Add the beer and simmer. Add the chiles and continue to simmer. Scoot the mixture over to one side of the pan and add the eggs. Cook over easy.

Dan Hislop
Weiser, Idaho

THE ADVENTURES OF
═══════ 'TWO-STORY TOM' ═══════

Look up 'character' in the dictionary and you'll find a picture of my old game warden buddy, Tom Whalen, aka 'Two-Story Tom'! There would be fewer people making a living by writing except for Tom and other folks like him. He just has 'material' written all over him. His nickname derives not from his stature 'cause in reality he falls into the vertically challenged category. But what he lacks in height, he makes up for in wind. So now you're wondering how he earned the moniker 'Two-Story Tom.' It happened around a campfire in deer camp. The second year Tom came to deer camp,

Tom rode up to camp, a distance of over 200 miles, with another friend named Mike. As bedtime neared, Tom was just finishing a story that he had started upon arriving three hours earlier. Tom puffed up with indignation when everyone began to rib him about being verbose. The matter was settled, though, when I asked Mike how many stories Tom had told him during the drive up. Mike scratched his head as he thought for a minute. "Just two," he answered. Tom didn't get a deer that year.

Tom didn't get a deer the first year he came to camp either. However, had he not told us himself, the rest of us would have never known about the tent pole he bagged that first year! My 14' x 16' wall tent has a single internal pole made out of a fence rail. The pole is situated about five feet inside the door (16' − 5' = 11'). The tent is big enough to comfortably sleep four guys and leave room for the kitchen and woodstove. On the night in question, three of the four occupants were dead to the world after slogging through snow all day. Only Tom heard the pickup drive past camp around midnight. Tom quit fantasizing about big bucks, and his game warden training took over as he pondered what good someone would be up to in the middle of the night on Hungry Ridge! Sounds from the vehicle faded and Tom again pictured big bucks behind every tree in his mind.

Only a game warden knows the adrenaline rush provided by the report of a high power rifle in the middle of the night. The first rush precipitated the second. That is Tom struggling out of his sleeping bag and attempting to run outside. The tent did not collapse when Tom T-Boned the previously mentioned tent pole only because of his size and having a mere 11" to accelerate prior to impact. But even Tom's self-directed maniacal laughter didn't awaken Dan, Mike or me. Tom told us what happened the next morning before any of us noticed the wood grain impression on his forehead!

Over the years we've come to treasure the nights that Tom lays awake because the rest of us are able to sleep without self-administering sub-lethal doses of medicinal spirits. For a little guy, he can really snore! To suddenly wake in the middle of the night when Tom tunes up defines 'sudden fear'! The fleeting thought of an asthmatic grizzly bear having gained entrance to the tent does produce an adrenaline rush measurable on the Richter Scale!

After pondering the possible reasons for several years, there is now no question that Tom's sleep patterns contribute to his lack of success deer hunting. Dan, his partner no longer asks if Tom went to sleep on his stand, but instead asks how long it took him to get to sleep, and how long he slept. The deer have plenty of notice to stay out of range when Tom is out in the woods.

I would like to report that the Twentieth Century ended without Tom bagging a deer. But alas, Tom did pass up a chance at one of the nicest two points any of us in camp had ever seen. Since a picture is worth a thousand words, he left a photo of it on the campground signboard.

Hunting Camp 1999
Penny Welch Photo

Soups, Stews & Chili

───── Bean and Potato Soup ─────

Ingredients:

1 cup Anasazi beans
1 lb. leftover ham chunks
2 potatoes, diced
1 onion, diced
2 ribs celery, diced
Seasonings to taste

Soak beans overnight. Put beans in pot and add water to more than cover the beans. Add ham chunks and simmer for 1 ½ hours. Add the diced vegetables and seasoning. Cook until vegetables are tender. Add liquid whenever needed for desired consistency. Serve with corn muffins.

───── Black Bean Chili ─────

Ingredients:

1 lb. ground meat
1 small onion, chopped
2-3 cloves garlic, minced
1 19 oz. can black bean soup
1 15 oz. can black beans, drained
1 cup medium, or hot, chunky salsa
1 ½ cups water

Brown meat, onion, and garlic. Drain off fat. Stir in soup, beans, salsa, and water. At home, bring to boil, reduce heat and simmer, uncovered, 15-20 minutes. In camp, prepare in a Dutch oven. Cover and set the Dutch in the firepan with 6-8 briquets underneath and 14-16 on the lid and cook for 15-20 minutes. May garnish with green onions, sour cream, cheese, or cilantro. Serves 4.

Bill Beck
Charlotte, North Carolina

Cajun Sausage Soup

Ingredients:

1 ½ lbs. mixed sausages, cut into ½ inch rounds
      (Italian, Polish, Cajun, etc.)
3 Tbsp. olive oil
2 large onions, sliced
2 large leeks, sliced
3-5 cloves garlic, pressed or finely minced
3-4 cans Cajun style stewed tomatoes
1 green bell pepper, chipped
3 small zucchini, sliced into ½ inch rounds
2 medium carrots, thinly sliced
1 small can garbanzo beans, drained
1 ½ cups dry red wine
8-9 cups beef stock
1 tsp. Cajun Dust™ seasoning
½ tsp. oregano
½ tsp. sweet basil
½ tsp. ground pepper
Salt to taste
3 Tbsp. fresh parsley, finely chopped
1-10 oz. thin pasta, cut into short lengths
Parmesan cheese, for each serving

Saute sausage in large skillet until lightly browned. Drain well. In a large soup pot, saute onions, leeks, and garlic in oil over medium to high heat until limp. Add all remaining ingredients, except pasta and Parmesan cheese. Simmer slowly for 1 hour. Add pasta and continue simmering ½ hour. Serve with Parmesan cheese sprinkled on top.

Tom Beck
Dolores, Colorado

95

Forty Mile Stew

I first sampled '40 Mile Stew' on a float trip down Middle Fork of Salmon River twenty years ago! Kent Ball, a co-worker pulled the fixin's out of a cooler and set to work while another fellow and I set up the firepan and dug charcoal out of a dry box. As Kent told the story, an old-time river guide said he fixed this when he was about forty miles down river. I've since heard another old-time river guide said he could make another forty miles after a meal of this stew. I'm not sure which of these old timers told the truth, but I do know this fills folks up at day's end! Here is my version of Kent's recipe.

Ingredients:
2-3 lb. round steak, cut into 1" cubes
2 lbs. breakfast sausage, made into patties
1/2 lb. mushrooms, sliced
1/4 cup olive or salad oil
3 lbs. potatoes, sliced 1/3" thick
2 large slicing tomatoes, sliced 1/3" thick
1/2 lb. green peppers, julienne
1 large yellow onion, sliced 1/3" thick
Seasonings
1 lb. sharp cheddar, sliced thick
       (use Swiss or Provolone, if you wish)

Using your camp stove or 15-18 briquets, brown the meat cubes in a 12" DO. Just as the meat finishes browning, throw the mushrooms in. Remove from heat and make sure none of the meat cubes have stuck to the bottom. Layer the potatoes slices over the meat and season to taste with salt, pepper, or your favorite camp seasoning. (Kent would add a dash of steak sauce for more flavor.) In whatever order you like, layer the tomatoes, peppers, and onions. Place the sausage patties over top of the last veggie. Bake slowly with 6-8 briquets underneath and 15-18 on top. Add fresh charcoal after an hour and cook for another 30-40 minutes. With only the moisture that cooks out of the vegetables for liquid, this ends up being more like a casserole than what we typically think of as a stew. Ten minutes before you're ready to serve, remove the charcoal from the lid, place the cheese slices over the sausage patties and replace the lid. The cheese slices will melt in about 5 minutes. Make sure when you serve that you get part of each layer.

Words of Wisdom

When you pack your duffel always plan on extremes of weather. Though it's been 90 + degrees for three weeks. Be prepared! Leave your rain gear and extra warm clothes at home and just wait, the weather will change for the worse.

Chicken Corn Chowder

Ingredients:

2 family-size cans cream of chicken soup
1 small onion, chopped
1 small jar (2 oz.) diced pimentos
4 medium potatoes, peeled, cut into ¾-1" cubes
2 cans pre-cut chicken (3.5 oz. cans), mixed or breast
1 can cream-style corn
1 can whole kernel corn
2 cups milk
1 tsp. pepper
¼ tsp. salt
¼ tsp celery salt
Other desired seasonings
Longhorn cheddar cheese, grated

Put all ingredients into large pan or Dutch oven. Cook until potatoes are cooked through and tender. Serve with grated cheese on top.

Debbie Osteen
Round Top, Texas

Dutch Oven Stew

Ingredients:

2 lbs. beef chuck, cut into 1" chunks
1 lb. pork sausage
1 clove garlic, minced
3 medium onions, sliced
2 bay leaves
1 Tbsp. salt
2 Tbsp. pepper
6 carrots, sliced
4 taters, cubed
2 green peppers, cubed
6 tomatoes, cubed
½ lb. cheddar cheese, shredded

Brown beef and sausage. Drain. Add 2 cups hot water and the rest of the stuff except cheese. Cook in a Dutch oven for about an hour. Add cheese just before serving. Feed bay leaves to coyotes. You eat the rest.

Mark Armbruster
Idaho Fish & Game
Challis, Idaho

Butch taking a bite for the camera
Penny Welch Photo

Southwest Green Chili
and Chicken Soup

Ingredients:

1 chicken, cut up
8 quarts water, boiling, for cooking the chicken
¼ cup olive oil
1 large onion, chopped
4 cloves garlic, minced or 1 Tbsp. garlic salt
Fresh ground pepper to taste
Salt to taste
10 cups chicken stock
2 cans chopped green chiles (8 oz.)
1/3 cup flour
¾ cup cold milk
2 cups Monterey Jack cheese, shredded
1 Tbsp. fresh cilantro, finely chopped

Place chicken in boiling water. Return to boiling. Cover, reduce heat to low, and simmer until chicken is tender, approximately 30 minutes. Remove chicken from pot, cool, remove skin and bones, and cut into 1 inch pieces. In a medium stockpot, sauté onion in olive oil until tender. Add garlic, pepper, salt, chicken stock, chilies, and chicken. Simmer 15 minutes. Whisk flour and milk together. Add to pot to thicken. Simmer 5 minutes and remove from heat. Add cheese, stirring constantly until cheese is melted and soup is thick and creamy. Add cilantro and serve with tortilla chips on the side.

Tom Beck
Dolores, Colorado

Camp clowns...
Catfish & CW on Dolores
River, Colorado
C.W. Welch Photo

Catfish Stew

Ingredients:

2 lbs. skinned catfish fillets, fresh or frozen
5 slices of bacon

Thaw fillets if frozen. Cut in 1 1/2 inch pieces. Fry bacon in Dutch oven over low heat until crisp. Drain on absorbent paper; crumble and set aside.

* * * * *

1 1/2 cup chopped onion
1 28 oz. can tomatoes, undrained
1/8 tsp. pepper, freshly ground
1 8 oz. can tomato sauce
3 cups diced Idaho potatoes
2 Tbsp. Worcestershire sauce
2 tsp. salt
1/4 tsp. hot pepper sauce

Add onion to Dutch oven; cover and cook 5 minutes or until tender. Stir in remaining ingredients. Bring to a boil; simmer 30 minutes. Add bacon and catfish. Cover and simmer 8-10 minutes or until fish flakes easily when tested with a fork. Serves 6.

Herb Pollard

Brian with the makin's for a
catfish stew
C.W. Welch Photo

Pen's Lentil Soup

Lentils abound here in North Central Idaho. The Palouse region, which encompasses parts of Idaho and eastern Washington, is billed the "Lentil Capitol of the World." Whether that's actually true or not, I don't know. What I do know is this. We enjoy a great variety of locally produced lentils. My wife created this recipe one winter day, and it's become a favorite, especially on those cool, gloomy days when fog banks hang halfway down the timbered ridges and the best spot in the house is being backed up to the woodstove.

Ingredients:

> 1 cup brown lentils, soaked for several hours
> or overnight, then rinsed thoroughly

Bring soaked lentils to a boil in twice the water to cover, then add:

> 6 slices bacon, diced into 1/4 " pieces
> 4-6 cloves garlic, minced
> 1 large onion, minced
> 4-6 ribs celery, diced or chopped fine
> 1 15 oz. can garlic and herb tomato sauce
> 2 cups fresh spinach, chopped
> 1 1/2 tsp. coarse ground pepper
> 3/4 tsp. garlic salt
> 4 tsp. sun dried tomato mustard, if available, or
> 3 tsp. ketchup
> 1 tsp. yellow mustard
> 1 ½ tsp. horseradish or creamed horseradish

Add water to cover ingredients and simmer until all fresh vegetables are cooked.

Penny Welch
Grangeville, Idaho

Round Top, Texas Beans

My wife, Penny, and I fixed this recipe in large quantities the fall of 1999 when we cooked for the Old Depot Antiques Fall Show. We made this in our deep 14" Dutch ovens so you will want to cut it in half for a regular 12" Dutch.

Ingredients:

4 cups pinto beans, soaked overnight
3 ham hocks
2 medium yellow onions, diced
1 tsp. Tabasco®, or other hot pepper sauce
10 cloves garlic, finely diced
1 tsp. cumin

Place beans in the Dutch oven with enough water to cover plus another two cups. Stir in remaining ingredients and simmer. We used 8-10 briquets underneath the Dutch and the same number on top. Stir occasionally and add a little more water if necessary. Freshen charcoal after 1 ½ hours. Total cooking time about 2-2 ½ hours. The longer they cook, the better they get! Serve with some fresh chopped onions, sliced jalapenos, and more hot sauce on the side for garnishments. We discovered that some Texans liked them with a splash of vinegar, and still others liked them with a little sugar sprinkled on top.

Cooking at Old Depot Antiques, Round Top, Texas.
Fall 1999   Penny Welch Photo

Kielbasa Stew

This recipe came about after being contacted by a health inspector in another state. Their regulations allowed only the use of weiners and Polish sausage unless a screened-in serving area was available. Thus, we have included more recipes containing kielbasa. Stews can take a while to cook when starting with larger chunks of meat. However, by using pre-cooked Polish sausage, this stew can be done in a very short time.

Ingredients:

1 pkg. German or Polish sausage
　　　cut into bite-size pieces
Carrots cut into bite-size pieces
2 medium onions sliced
5-6 ribs celery cut into bite-size pieces
1-16 oz. pkg. frozen brussels sprouts
　　　or 2 cups fresh, if in season
2 turnips, cut into chunks
2 parsnips, cut into chunks
6 medium potatoes, red or white, cut into chunks
Salt/pepper/seasonings

Put all ingredients into 12" Dutch oven. Add liquid. Apply heat and simmer at least until all vegetables are tender.

Butch serving samples after doing a cooking demonstration at Itchycoo Park '99 Summer 1999 Penny Welch Photo

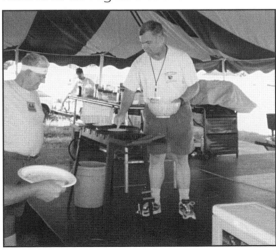

Tom's Chicken Stock

Ingredients:

2 chickens, cut into large pieces
8 quarts water
3 ribs celery, with leaves
2 onions, quartered
2-3 cloves garlic, minced
6 sprigs fresh parsley
2-3 leeks, white and light green parts
2 bay leaves
1 doz. peppercorns
4 whole allspice balls
1 Tbsp. thyme
2-3 Tbsp. salt, regular or sea salt

Wash chickens in cold water and place in large stockpot. Add water and all remaining ingredients. Partially cover (for a clear broth) and simmer approximately 1 hour . Remove from heat and cool to room temperature. Remove the chicken pieces. Discard all the whole seasoning and vegetables, leaving only the chicken and the broth. Chill broth in the refrigerator until fat solidifies on the surface. Remove the fat and discard. Remove the chicken meat from the bones. Return meat to broth and reheat for chicken soup. For freezing, chicken may be frozen separately from the broth, or return to the broth and freeze.

Tom Beck
Dolores, Colorado

Words of Wisdom

Get your wood and water packed during the daylight hours if at all possible. Trying to navigate with a flashlight in your mouth and your arms full usually results in a preventable accident!

VEGETABLES and SALADS

VEGGIES FOR CAMP

Keeping fresh produce in camp requires some planning, especially if you have to plan for salad hounds. Consider taking cabbage and making coleslaw instead of lettuce. The cabbage will keep several times longer than lettuce. A couple of years ago we shredded cabbage for coleslaw and packed it in resealable bags for a river trip. Squeeze as much air out as possible before you seal it. On day five we popped open the bags and made the dressing and had fresh slaw in less than ten minutes. If soups or stews are on your menu, throw in a few turnips and parsnips. Like potatoes, carrots, and onions they will keep fresh in a cooler or pack box for several days without ice. If you don't grow a garden, stop if you can at the local farmers' market on your way out of town on a summer trip. Farm fresh veggies taste better and are better for you. I try to keep canned veggies to a minimum just to save weight in my garbage sack. Also taking fresh veggies instead of frozen ones will reduce the amount of money you spend on ice. Depending on how long your trip is, many fresh veggies can be peeled, sliced, diced, etc., at home, which also saves preparation time in camp and reduces your garbage to bring out.

Blue Cheese Dressing

Ingredients:

2 cups Hellman's® mayonnaise
½ small slab Danish blue cheese
1 clove garlic, pressed or finely minced
Milk, as needed

Mix mayonnaise, blue cheese, and garlic together, adding milk to thin to desired consistency.

Sandy Riney
Las Piedras Ranch
Real County, Texas

Asparagus Spears

Ingredients:

1 lb. asparagus spears, trimmed
1 cup cooking liquid,
    white wine, chicken broth, or water
Butter
Seasonings
Parmesan Cheese

Place asparagus spears and liquid in a Dutch oven and cook for approximately 15 minutes or until tender. Drain and add a little butter and seasonings. Sprinkle Parmesan cheese on top, if desired.

Words of Wisdom

If possible segregate items by use or refrigeration needs, i.e. dry goods, frozen stuff, drinks, and fresh produce.

Save leftover spice containers with screw on lids for your camp spices.

Boiled Spuds & Veggies

Ingredients:

Red potatoes, whole if small, halved or quartered
    if larger
Pearl onions. peeled
Butter
Parsley, chopped

Boil potatoes in water until they begin to soften, or about three-quarters done. Add the pearl onions and cook until potatoes and onions are nearly done. Drain potatoes and onions. Add chopped parsley. Add butter and melt over hot vegetables, stirring to coat with butter and parsley.

Fancy Cranberries

Ingredients:

1 can cranberries, whole berries
Cinnamon and/or nutmeg
3/4 cup fresh apple, chopped

Heat cranberries in a small Dutch oven. Season with cinnamon, nutmeg, or other desired spices. Add chopped apples and simmer on a low heat until apples are tender.

Cucumber and Tomato Salad

Ingredients:

4 cucumbers, cubed or sliced
3 tsp. salt
1 cup half and half
1 tsp. sugar
1 tsp. pepper
1 tsp. dill weed
4 tsp. vinegar
1 large tomato, diced, or
   1 cup cherry tomatoes, halved

Sprinkle salt on cucumbers and let sit for 1 to 1 1/2 hours while cucumbers sweat. Add water to cukes, rinse and drain off liquid. In a separate bowl, stir half and half, sugar, pepper, dill weed, and vinegar. Pour over the cucumbers, add tomatoes, and gently stir. Let chill for an hour to let flavors blend. This creamed vegetable dish provides color, variety and flavor to summer entrees.

Penny Welch
Grangeville, Idaho

Broccoli Salad

Ingredients:

2 bunches broccoli, chopped fine including stem
1/3 cup chopped red onion
1/3 cup yellow raisins
½ cup roasted, salted, sunflower seeds
½ lb. bacon, fried crisp and crumbled, optional

Dressing:

1 cup mayonnaise
¼ cup sugar
2 tsp. vinegar

Mix dressing ingredients and set in refrigerator for four hours. Mix dressing with broccoli and other ingredients and serve.

Sue Kinner
Grangeville, Idaho

Caesar Salad

Ingredients:

1 head Romaine lettuce
1 small purple onion, thinly sliced into rings
1 small can anchovies
1 package croutons
To taste, hard Parmesan cheese, grated
Caesar dressing

Tear lettuce leaves into bite-sized pieces into a large bowl. Add onions and anchovies and lightly toss. Grate as much parmesan cheese into the salad as desired and toss into salad. Put croutons on top of salad. Serve with favorite prepared Caesar dressing.

Coleslaw

Ingredients:

1/2 head cabbage, shredded or chopped
3/4 cup mayonnaise
1/2 cup half and half, milk, or evaporated milk
1/2 tsp. pepper, fresh ground if possible
1/2 tsp. salt
2 1/2 tsp. sugar
4 tsp. vinegar
1/8 tsp. paprika

Place cabbage in a large bowl. Mix all other ingredients in a smaller bowl until smooth and creamy. Pour over the cabbage and stir to coat the cabbage thoroughly. Chill, stir, and serve. Additional paprika may be sprinkled on top for color.

Penny Welch
Grangeville, Idaho

I admit that I wasn't much of a coleslaw fan until my wife made this for me the first time. Given my choice now, I prefer slaw over green salad.

Green Beans and More

Ingredients:

3-4 cups fresh green beans
2-3 slices bacon, diced
4-6 mushrooms, sliced

Put green beans and bacon into 10" Dutch oven. Add water, stock or white wine for cooking liquid. Cover and simmer 10-15 minutes or until beginning to become tender. Remove lid and add mushrooms. Continue to cook until thoroughly cooked, about 5-10 minutes. May be cooked by using about 10 briquets under the DO or cook on top of the cook stove.

— Green Beans with Red Peppers —

Ingredients:

Fresh green beans
Red pepper, coarsely chopped
Other vegetables, if desired

Put green beans and red pepper pieces into 10" Dutch oven. Add water, stock or white wine for cooking liquid. Cover and simmer 15-20 minutes or until tender. May be cooked by using about 10 briquets under the DO or cook on top of the cook stove.

———— Four-Five Bean Salad ————

Ingredients:

1 can kidney beans, drained
1 can wax beans, drained
1 can green beans, drained
1 can garbanzo beans, drained
1 can black-eyed peas, drained, (optional)
1 medium onion, sliced
1 green pepper, sliced into rings
½ cup sugar
½ cup vinegar
½ cup salad oil
1 tsp. salt
½ tsp. dry mustard
½ tsp. dried tarragon, crushed
2 Tbsp. parsley

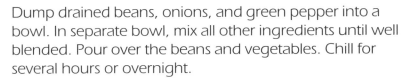

Dump drained beans, onions, and green pepper into a bowl. In separate bowl, mix all other ingredients until well blended. Pour over the beans and vegetables. Chill for several hours or overnight.

Dick Kirtner
Little Cabin, Bartlett-Hopkins Ranch
South Fork of Clearwater River

Garden Fresh
Chicken Pasta Salad

When you're grilling chicken breasts for another recipe, do 3-4 extra and try this dish for a change of pace. It makes a quick dish when you want a "lite" dinner or lunch.

Ingredients:

3-4 chicken breasts, grilled and seasoned to taste,
   cut into 1" squares
1 12 oz. pkg. vegetable rotini
1/2 can black olives, sliced
1/2 cup green olives, sliced, optional
1/2 small purple onion, diced
1 cucumber or zucchini, diced into ½" cubes
3-4 large mushrooms, sliced
2 Roma tomatoes, diced
½ green or red bell pepper, diced
1 tsp. salt
4-6 Tbsp. olive oil
½ cup vinegar
Ground black pepper to taste

Cook pasta according to package directions, rinse, and chill in fridge or cooler. Put veggies in a bowl and add salt and toss. Let veggies rest for 15-20 minutes. Add oil, vinegar, pasta, pepper, and chicken. Gently toss. Let salad rest for about 30 minutes stirring occasionally. Serve with a side of garlic or French bread.

Words of Wisdom

Keep some large plastic garbage bags in your camp kitchen. If it rains they can be pressed into service for rain ponchos and to put items like sacks of charcoal in so they don't get wet. When using garbage bags as rain gear **DON'T** use them for small children under age 12.

——Sweet and Sour Red Cabbage——

Ingredients:

1 hard red cabbage
1 ½ tsp. butter
5-6 sweet red apples, chopped fine
½ cup vinegar

Shred cabbage and wash in colander. Melt butter in Dutch oven. Add apples and fry for 10-15 minutes before adding cabbage. Set Dutch oven in fire pan with 8-10 briquets underneath and 15 on the lid and cook for about 15-20 minutes. Add vinegar and cook until cabbage is tender.

Penne Pasta with Roasted ———— Vegetables ————

Ingredients:

1 lb. plum tomatoes, cut into 1" pieces
2 medium bell pepper, cut into ½" strips
2 small zucchini, or yellow squash,
   cut into strips or slices
1 medium onion, chopped
1 tsp. salt
½ tsp. pepper
½ cup bottled pesto sauce
½ lb. penne pasta
Parmesan cheese

Mix vegetables, seasonings and 2 tablespoons of the pesto sauce. Bake in Dutch oven for 20-30 minutes. Cook pasta and drain, reserving 2 tablespoons water. Toss in remaining pesto sauce. Add vegetables and serve with Parmesan cheese. Serves 4-6.

Bill Beck
Charlotte, North Carolina

Stuffed Tomatoes

Ingredients:

4 large tomatoes
2 cups cottage cheese
Fresh parsley or cilantro, chopped
Ground pepper/seasonings

Remove the stem from the tomatoes. Slice in half from top down, not cutting all the way through to the bottom of the tomato. Cut additionally into quarters, sixths, or eights, depending on the size of the tomatoes. Parsley or cilantro, and other seasonings, may be mixed with the cottage cheese before stuffing into tomatoes; or, stuff the tomatoes with the unseasoned cottage cheese adding the garnishments on top.

Summer Red Potato Salad

Ingredients:

3 lbs. red potatoes
1 doz. eggs
3-4 baby dill pickles, chopped
1 can olives, chopped or sliced
4 celery ribs, chopped
1 purple onion, chopped
1 cup salad dressing, such as Miracle Whip®
1/4 cup mustard
4 Tbsp. cilantro or parsley, chopped
1/3-1/2 cup dill pickle juice

Boil the red potatoes and cool. Hard boil the eggs and cool. Cut the red potatoes and eggs into 1/2-3/4 inch cubes and put in a large container that has a lid. Add all other ingredients to potatoes and eggs. Put lid on container. Toss ingredients to mix thoroughly. Chill and serve. Serves 10-12.

Howard's
—— Cucumber and Onion Salad ——

Ingredients:

2-3 cucumbers, sliced paper thin
1 medium onion, white or purple, sliced into thin rings
1 green bell pepper, sliced into rings, optional
1-2 cups mayonnaise
1-2 cups water
1 cup vinegar
1-1 ½ cups sugar
3-4 tsp. salt
1-3 tsp. coarse ground pepper
¼-½ cup olive

Place cucumbers and onions in a bowl. Add cold water to cover, and let chill for at least an hour. For the dressing, in a separate bowl, combine the mayonnaise, water, vinegar, sugar, salt, and ground pepper. The sauce will taste sweet. Drain the chilled cucumbers and onions and fold in the sauce, covering all the vegetables. Add the olive oil and mix in. Chill for another hour or more, the longer the better, to blend the flavors before serving.

Howard Konetzke, Jr.
La Grange, Texas

Howard getting
"prettied up"
Penny Welch Photo

115

DRY CAMPS

It doesn't matter whether you backpack or rough it in the luxury of a $100,000.00 RV, water and its availability impacts every camping trip. It's one thing to watch news reports about water shortages somewhere in the country but it hits home when you pull into your favorite campground late at night to see a sign at the entrance which reads "No Potable Water" or worse yet, "No Water Available"! It's impossible to plan for every eventuality but without water just about everything grinds to a halt.

When you're loading up before the trip, take as much water as practical given space and weight considerations. At the very least invest in two or three collapsible water jugs. If you find yourself in a campground without water you can at least backtrack to a place where water is available.

If camping where there is no water, you're limited by the capacity of your RV's water tank or how many water jugs you hauled from home. In these instances water conservation becomes a concern for everyone in camp! Without becoming anal retentive there are lots of things you can do to cut water consumption. The most important is to simply make everyone aware of the situation. As an added incentive, anyone caught 'wasting' water gets assigned to make the next trip back down the road for more water!

Here are strategies I've used over the years to conserve water. Unless I'm cooking for a large group I use one meal's rinse water for the next meal's wash water. Heat one basin of water for everyone to wash up with before supper. You can also take the last of the morning's coffee and rinse off the breakfast dishes. That evening when you get back to camp wipe them with a moistened dishcloth to which you've added a couple of drops of dish soap. Rinse them in the water you heat up for hand washing and they're ready for supper. Even in cooking you can use the same water for two things. Say for instance you're having pasta and steamed broccoli. Drain the pasta into another pot and use the same water for steaming your broccoli. A little common sense will do a lot to stretch your water.

Other steps you can take include boiling, filtering and/or purifying non-potable water. Check large sporting goods stores and outdoor catalog outlets to locate water filters. The extra money that a filter costs and the effort required to filter enough water for drinking, cooking, and brushing your teeth is worth it!

I grew up drinking out of springs and live streams. When Dad and I fished our favorite "cricks" in SE Idaho, we regularly quenched our thirst literally at our feet. Our only concern was getting upstream beyond where domestic livestock grazed! Unfortunately water quality goes down when man, in the name of progress, intensifies his use of the land and the water. In many cases the water may appear to be of the same quality as when Dad and I drank it years ago, but of course it's the little critters that you can't see in the water which are the problem. Before you head for the woods, stop at the drugstore and pick up a small bottle of iodine from the pharmacist. Add two drops of iodine per quart of water and let set overnight before drinking. If you have enough water from home or enough filtered water for drinking, treat non-potable water with iodine for dish washing and other cleanup chores.

Thinking ahead and attempting to plan for the unexpected takes the worry out of the water problem!

Soaking at Barth
Hot springs
Main Salmon 1998

Welch Photo
Collection

Janie's Taters

Ingredients:

> 1 small onion, chopped
> 2-3 Tbsp. butter
> 4-6 slices bacon
> 1 pkg. frozen hash browns
> 2 cups cream of chicken soup
> 1 pint sour cream
> 2 cups grated cheddar cheese
> 1 cube butter, melted
> 3 cups crushed corn flakes

In advance, precook the onion in the butter; fry the bacon, drain, and crumble. Place the onion and bacon in a 12 inch Dutch oven and add the hash browns, soup, sour cream , ½ the cheese, and ¾ of the cube of butter. Mix all ingredients and bake at about 350 for 1 hour, using 4-6 under the oven and 16-18 on the lid. Then add the rest of the butter, cheese, and the corn flakes and continue to cook for another ½ hour.

Janie Carrico
Twin Falls, Idaho

Marie's Green Beans

Ingredients:

> 2-3 slices bacon, fried crisp and crumbled
> ¼ onion, diced
> 1 can green beans, drained, saving the juice

Bring the juice from the green beans and the bacon to a boil. Add the diced onions and the green beans. Cook for ten minutes.

Marie Mathis
Somerville, Texas

Marinated Vegetables

Vegetables:

    4 stalks fresh broccoli, chopped
    8 large fresh mushrooms, chopped
    1 medium size green pepper, chopped
    3 stalks celery, chopped, reserving leaves
    1 small head cauliflower, broken into florets
    3 carrots, sliced
    Cherry tomatoes

Combine all vegetables, except tomatoes, and toss lightly.

Dressing Ingredients:

    3/4 cup sugar
    2 tsp. dry mustard
    1 tsp. salt
    2/3 cup vinegar
    1 1/2 cup vegetable oil
    1 small onion, quartered
    2 Tbsp. poppy seeds

Combine remaining ingredients in blender, mix well and pour over vegetables. Garnish with celery leaves and cherry tomatoes. Chill at least 3 hours. Serves 10-12.

This is a great dish to serve when you're cooking for a large group. It fills in for a salad and you don't have to have different choices of dressing to please everyone.

Words of Wisdom

Make your own fire starting aids. Take a cardboard egg carton and place a tablespoon of sawdust or wood shavings in each indentation. Melt some wax in a tin can and press the top together to form a spout. Pour a little wax over each pile of sawdust. You can tear them apart for individual use.

CULINARY BOMBS

While being a game warden for over twenty years, it was my good fortune to be invited into many camps. Of course I ended up being an uninvited guest in many others, but I will save those stories for later. Anyway...I couldn't come close to putting a number on how many camp cooks I've crossed paths with over the years, but it for sure numbers in the hundreds. As you might expect, the skill level of these cooks runs the gamut from totally inexperienced to a chef who quit the big time and went to work for a wilderness outfitter to escape the concrete jungle.

It's probably safe to say that many of these cooks began their camp cooking education with a wiener on a stick or a can of stew set in the coals at the edge of an open fire. Properly done, you can cook canned goods without a pot and save having to wash some dishes. Improperly done, however... you might end up with beans on your face!

As taught to me when I was a Boy Scout, cooking in cans is simple and easy. Even now these many years later, I will occasionally heat a vegetable up in a can if all my DO's are in use. To do this, I merely take a can opener and pierce the top in three or four places on the top, then set it on a couple of small coals right at the edge of the fire. As liquid begins to bubble out the openings, I turn the can a quarter turn with a pair of leather gloves. I keep turning the can until liquid has bubbled out of each of the three or four holes that I put in the top. This allows for even distribution of heat and prevents burning the contents.

I can't emphasize enough that the top of the can must be pierced before you apply heat to the can! The openings allow pressure to escape as the contents begin to cook. Failure to provide for the release of pressure will in a very short time result in a 'Culinary Bomb' proportional to the size of the can and how much heat was being applied!

A fellow officer responded to a call a couple of years ago to a site along the Little Salmon River in Central Idaho where some subjects were reported to be fishing with 'Dupont Spinners'! For those of you who do not know, a 'Dupont Spinner' consists of one or more sticks of dynamite, or similar explosive, deposited into the water. The explosion in the water stuns the fish, which allows for them to be retrieved merely by using a net. Needless to say, such actions are contrary to regulations and constitute a major violation.

When Roy arrived at the riverbank campsite where the explosions had been reported, evidence of the explosions was readily visible. The rookie cook in this camp had set two family size cans of chili con carne with beans in the fire and **had not pierced the tops of the cans!** Not only did dinner turn out to be a 'bomb,' But he had to endure ridicule from his buddies and a grin from the game warden!

Chris Wood & CeeDub kick back after fixing brunch and getting "bombed" at Van Cleave Ranch Sept. 1998
Penny Welch Photo

Sauerkraut Salad

Ingredients:

1/2 cup vinegar
2 cups sugar
2 medium-size cans or packages of sauerkraut,
   if cans, the kraut may be rinsed
   in a colander before use
1 cup celery, chopped
1 cup onion, chopped
1 green pepper, chopped

Dissolve vinegar and sugar. Bring to boil and cool. Pour over sauerkraut which has been drained. Mix chopped celery onion, and green pepper into sauerkraut. Place in refrigerator for at least 24 hours. Serve this with barbequed brisket for a great color and taste combination.

Steamed Sweet Potatoes

Ingredients:

4-6 sweet potatoes or yams, washed
Small amount of salad oil
Water as cooking liquid

Wash the sweet potatoes or yams thoroughly and pat dry. Rub a small amount of salad oil on the skins to coat them. Place on a rack in a 12" Dutch oven and add liquid on the bottom for steaming. Cook with 8-10 briquets on the bottom and about 20 briquets on the lid. Bake for 45 minutes or until pierced easily with a fork.

I know it sounds corny, but try this before you pass judgment. Take leftover sweet potatoes and cut them into ¾ inch cubes. Fry them as you would hash browns, using a little butter, if desired. Season with salt and pepper to taste.

Tomato Basil Salad

Ingredients:

Sliced tomatoes
1 clove garlic per tomato, chopped fine
Feta cheese
Olive oil
Chopped basil

Arrange sliced tomatoes on plate, and sprinkle garlic on them. Crumble feta cheese over tomatoes. Drizzle olive oil over the tomatoes and sprinkle with chopped basil.

Sandy Riney
Las Piedras Ranch
Real County, Texas

Words of Wisdom

Keep a permanent marking pen in your chuck box to mark leftovers and anything not packaged in its original container.

Italian Squash

Ingredients:

1 zucchini squash, sliced
1 yellow squash, sliced
1 red pepper, cut into strips or rounds
3-4 cloves garlic, minced
3-4 Tbsp. olive oil
Seasonings to taste
Parmesan cheese

Brown vegetables and garlic in olive oil. Season and cook until tender. Sprinkle with Parmesan cheese.

Sandy Riney
Las Piedras Ranch
Real County, Texas

Lime Cucumbers

Ingredients:

4-6 cucumbers
Juice from 3 limes
2 Tbsp. dill weed

Peel cucumbers and cut into slices, finger food size. Place in a container that can be covered and refrigerated. Dribble lime juice over the cucumbers. Sprinkle dill weed over the cucumbers. Let the cucumbers marinate in the juice and toss intermittently to distribute lime juice and dill. Serve as finger food before dinner or as a side dish. A few grinds of fresh black pepper will give these cucumber spears a little more zing!

Words of Wisdom

Keep firewood covered at night if possible. Should it rain during the night the first person up will have an easier time getting the fire going.

Rainbow Rice

Ingredients:

4 bags of pre-measured rice, or rice for a serving
    of 8-12, prepared ahead of time
2 Tbsp. salad oil
1 can black olives, sliced
1 red pepper, sliced and diced
1 green pepper, sliced and diced
1 purple onion, sliced and diced
2 Roma tomatoes, sliced and diced
Seasoned rice vinegar
Olive oil

Prepare rice with salad oil. Rinse thoroughly in a strainer to prevent clumping, and cool. In a large bowl, place cooled rice. Fold in olives, red and green peppers, onions, and tomatoes. Dress with the seasoned rice vinegar and olive oil.

Twice-Baked Potatoes

First, prepare potatoes by baking, using your oven at home, or in a Dutch oven using the following method.

> 6-8 Idaho potatoes, washed,
>   and brushed with shortening
> Enough small cleaned pebbles, 3/4-1"
>   diameter, to keep potatoes from
>   touching bottom of the Dutch oven.

Cover pebbles with water (one inch in bottom of Dutch oven). Place potatoes on the pebbles. Cover and place 6-8 briquets on bottom and 18-20 briquets on the lid. Bake one hour.

Ingredients:

1 cube butter, melted
1/2-3/4 cup milk
2-3 tsp. fresh chives, chopped
Salt/pepper/seasonings
3/4 cup grated cheese
Sour cream, or other garnishments, if desired

Let the potatoes cool until easily handled. Halve the potatoes lengthwise and scoop out the insides of the potatoes from the skins into a bowl. Reserve skins to be used as shells. Mash the potatoes, adding melted butter, milk, chopped fresh chives, and other seasonings. Spoon the mashed potatoes back into the shells and place in a Dutch oven on the pebbles or a rack, no liquid added, with 6-8 briquets under the oven and about 15 briquets on the lid. Heat for about 10-15 minutes. Remove lid and sprinkle grated cheese on top. Replace lid and continue heating for about another 5 minutes or until cheese is melted. Serve with sour cream and other garnishments.

Marinades & Rubs

MARINADES

I'm not sure when I first heard of marinades. I know my Mom didn't use them. Every chunk of meat went into a roasting pan or a skillet. Meat, potatoes, a vegetable, and a salad aptly described a typical menu around our house. Venison was treated the same way beef or pork. In the pan it went. In looking back now I realize my sisters and I grew up knowing venison tasted differently, but we didn't attach any special significance to that fact. As I grew older, I learned that some folks referred to this difference as a 'gamey' flavor and used marinades to mask or hide the taste of venison. I wish I had a dollar for every time I've heard someone describe marinating a piece of wild game then telling me there was no way you could tell it was venison after it was cooked. To my way of thinking they're missing the point.

Marinades can be used to tenderize and flavor any cut of meat whether it's venison or domestic. I prefer to use marinades to introduce different flavors rather than a mask to hide something.

Typically a marinade will be composed of at least two ingredients; an acid in the form of vinegar or citrus juice, and an oil. The acid acts as a tenderizing agent, and the oil carries the flavors of any added spices and seasonings. If you plan to grill the meat, the oil also protects against burning. Because of the acid, use a non-reactive container such as glass, plastic, ceramic or stainless steel. When possible, I use a self-sealing plastic bag, which reduces the amount of marinade needed.

Many of us, myself included, tend to operate under the philosophy 'a lot does a good job, more does it better!' Not necessarily so when it comes to marinades. Decide beforehand the purpose for your marinade and proceed accordingly. If you want to flavor something such as a venison back strap, do not marinate it over night, as you would do if trying to tenderize a beef brisket. The judicious use of marinades will add to your repertoire of interesting methods for preparing meat, be it domestic or wild.

Red Wine Marinade

Ingredients:

> ½ cup olive or vegetable oil
> ½ cup red wine (burgundy is my favorite)
> 1 tsp. coarse ground black pepper
> ½ tsp. sea salt
> 1 tsp. each of thyme, rosemary, and oregano

Change the combination of spices to suit your personal taste. Often, when I make this marinade, I use only rosemary. It's great for lamb or an elk roast.

Sweet & Sour Marinade

Ingredients:

> ½ cup olive or vegetable oil
> ¼ cup red wine vinegar
> ¼ cup honey
> 1 tsp. coarse ground black pepper
> 2 tsp. coarse diced celery
> 2 tsp. coarse chopped onion

—Cee Dub's Pepper Steak Marinade—

Ingredients:

> ½ cup red wine
> ½ cup olive oil
> 2 tsp. pickled jalapenos finely chopped
> (Use fresh jalapenos for additional heat!)
> 2 tsp. coarse ground black pepper
> 1 tsp. finely minced garlic

Whip this up and marinate steaks one hour before grilling or pan-frying. Make sure you turn the steaks a couple of times while their marinating.

—— Southwest Marinade ——

Ingredients:

½ cup olive or canola oil
1 cup cerveza (beer)
1 tsp. red wine vinegar
1 tsp. cumin
2 tsp. finely chopped cilantro
1 tsp. coarse ground black pepper
½ tsp. sea salt

"Soaking" up some rays on the Main Salmon 1998
Penny Welch Photo

—— Grilled Chicken Marinade ——

Ingredients:

½ cup olive or vegetable oil
½ cup dry white wine
1 tsp. apple cider vinegar
2 small green onions. finely diced
2 tsp. finely minced celery
½ tsp. sea salt
½ tsp. coarse ground black pepper
1 tsp. chopped rosemary

—— Basco's Teriyaki Marinade ——

Ingredients:

> 1 12 oz. bottle of soy sauce
> ½ cup brown sugar
> 1 cup water
> 6 cloves garlic, minced fine
> 2 Tbsp. finely minced fresh ginger

Place all ingredients in a sauce pan and bring to a boil. Allow to simmer for 5-10 minutes. Cool and store in refrigerator. Marinate any red meat or chicken for 1-2 hours prior to cooking.

Dave McGonigal
Idaho Fish & Game
Boise, Idaho

—— Cee Dub's Grill Marinade ——

Try this marinade with a venison loin roast you're going to grill.

Ingredients:

> 3 small jars of marinated artichoke hearts
> 6-8 cloves of garlic, finely minced
> ½ tsp. sea salt
> 1 tsp. coarse ground black pepper

Drain all the liquid from the artichoke hearts and transfer to a pint jar. (See the recipe for Middle Fork Choked Chicken and use the artichokes in it.) Add the other ingredients and let sit in the refrigerator for 3-4 days. Every time you reach in the fridge for a beer shake the marinade well. Place a 3-4 pound chunk of venison back strap in a re-sealable plastic bag and pour the marinade in. Let stand for 2-3 hours before you grill.

RUBS FOR MEAT, NOT BACKS

Another method for flavoring meats prior to cooking involves rubbing the meat with a mixture of seasonings and spices. Read on for more!

Along about my sophomore year in college, I learned that if I could wrangle a date with a nursing student after she'd completed a section on 'backrubs,' I stood a good chance of being the recipient of a practice session. I would be remiss if I didn't admit that on occasion these 'practice sessions' led to other preparations! However…as my cooking education progressed in later years, it dawned on me using a rub as defined in the culinary world made great foreplay when preparing some meat dishes!

The debate among folks who utilize rubs for preparing meats centers around salt! One school of thought contends that the salt draws out moisture that causes the meat to be tough. These folks rely on spices and herbs for the most part. The other folks use salt along with their choice of spices and herbs for flavor. Not being one to take sides, I've included recipes from both camps! If you have never used a rub, you can have a lot of fun experimenting with this technique!

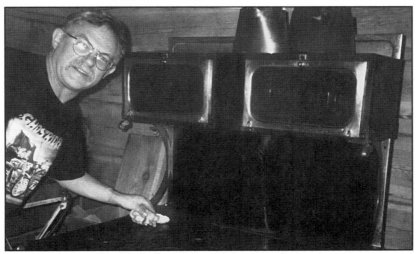

CeeDub "rubbing" his woodstove!
Penny Welch Photo

Cache Basin Sheep Rub

Riding into someone's camp while on a horse trip about suppertime occasionally results in an invitation for dinner. A successful sheep hunter and his pardner were just fixing to eat dinner one such evening when I pulled into an adjacent camp. They had packed their ram back into camp the day before, and had spent the day recuperating as they slow cooked a loin roast over a bed of Mountain Mahogany coals. Never one to pass up a chance to eat bighorn sheep, I took them up on their invitation. I've since used this on domestic lamb using fresh rosemary.

Ingredients:

2 tsp. dried rosemary
2 tsp. dried minced garlic
2 tsp. dried vegetable flakes
1 tsp. coarse ground black pepper
½ tsp. ground nutmeg

Words of Wisdom

If the weather looks bad fill a thermos with hot water at breakfast. Should someone go out of a boat or get caught in the rain this along with some instant soup will restore their humor and possibly stall off hypothermia.

South of the Border Rub

Ingredients:

1 tsp. ground cumin
1 tsp. chili powder
1 tsp. coriander seeds
1 tsp. fresh chopped cilantro
1 tsp. fresh chopped parsley
1 tsp. sea salt
1 tsp. coarse ground pepper

Howard's
———— Fish and Seafood Rub ————

Ingredients:

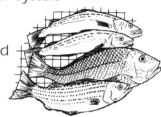

5-8 lbs. of catfish, shrimp, or oysters
2 cups corn meal
1 cup flour
1 tsp. pepper, finely ground
½ tsp. garlic powder
3-4 tsp. salt
Peanut oil for deep frying

Soak the fish or seafood in cold water. Mix all the dry ingredients in a large bowl or pan. Preheat the oil to about 350 degrees. Roll the fish or seafood pieces in the corn meal mixture and place them in the hot grease. Use a slotted spoon or tongs to turn the pieces, not a fork. Cook pieces until they are golden brown and float to the surface, approximately 3-6 minutes for fish, depending upon the size of the pieces of fish, and 2-3 minutes for shrimp and oysters.

Howard Konetzke, Jr.
La Grange, Texas

———— Beef Brisket Rub ————

Ingredients:

2 Tbsp. sweet paprika
1 Tbsp garlic powder
1 Tbsp. black pepper, coarsely ground
1 Tbsp. dried thyme
1 Tbsp. dried basil
1 Tbsp. dried parsley

Combine all ingredients in a small bowl and mix well. Apply rub to meat, ends included, and coat as thickly as possible.

Prime Rib Rub

Ingredients:

> 3-4 Tbsp. coarse ground pepper
> 2-3 tsp. garlic powder
> 2 tsp ground rosemary

Mix the pepper, garlic powder, and rosemary together. Rub this mixture onto the prime rib, thoroughly patting in the spices onto the meat.

Words of Wisdom

When planning your menus always plan on a little extra and have some emergency rations. An extra canned ham, dried beans and rice will make a great dinner if plans or weather changes to extend your stay.

Texas Barbecued Brisket Rub

Ingredients:

> Seasoning salt
> Garlic powder
> Ground pepper
> Yoshida's Original Gourmet Sauce®

Sprinkle dry seasonings listed above all over a 5-7 pound brisket. Rub thoroughly on the meat, coating quite heavily. Place meat uncovered, fat side down, in a barbeque and cook for 2-3 hours at 300-325 degrees. Using large-size, heavy aluminum foil, crisscross sheets on a flat surface. Remove brisket and place fat side up on the aluminum foil. Dribble about 3-5 tablespoons Yoshida's Original Gourmet Sauce® over the meat. Wrap up tightly in the aluminum foil so that it is completely covered. Place back in the barbeque for 3-4 hours at 325-350 degrees.

Howard Konetzke, Jr.
La Grange, Texas

FISH and FOWL

OYSTERS

Mention oysters and most folks conjure up images of oyster stew, fried oysters, smoked oysters, or oysters on the half shell. These denizens of the estuaries go by such names as Blue Point, Hood Canal, Malpeque, and Kumamoto, etc. We have here in the Rockies, oysters, in name only, that are known as 'Rocky Mountain Oysters' or, RMO's. Should individuals from the East (that portion of the US laying between Cheyenne, Wyoming and the Atlantic Ocean) read this they may have already asked themselves, "What is a Rocky Mountain Oyster"? In an effort to be politically correct, I'll phrase it like this! Male calves are relieved at sometime in their life of two 'items' that require they change their name from 'Joe Bull' to 'Joe Steer'! The next question one might ask is, "Where did they come from?" My guess is it went something like this. At some long distant branding fire, a chuck wagon cook ran short of real grub so he took a bucket of these 'items', rolled them in flour and fried them crisp. I'd also hazard a guess not everyone on the crew went back for seconds.

Call it a mental block, but Rocky Mountain Oysters rank very high on my list of non-preferred foods. But each to their own! Some folks consider them a delicacy of the first order. Here in Idaho one town bills its summer festival as the 'World's Largest Rocky Mountain Oyster Feed'! On the two occasions I've attended this celebration, I restricted myself to potato salad and liquid refreshments that come in 12 oz. brown bottles. In watching other attendees I also noticed many folks first consumed the contents of numerous 12 oz. brown bottles prior to getting in line for their first helping of RMO's. Could it be a lot of folks must make mental preparations before partaking of this 'pasture delicacy'?

My one and only personal experience occurred thirteen years ago about forty air miles north of the Mexican border in a little town just off I-10. At the time I'd just become our outfit's first full-time undercover investigator. A particular state that borders Mexico had an ongoing investigation and invited me down for some OJT (on-the-job training). Only those who've done UC work can truly appreciate the situations they might find themselves in. This includes such mundane things as eating and drinking!

For the purposes of this story, the guy I partnered up with for two weeks I'll call Jake. Jake, being a transplanted New Englander, knew at the time more about oysters than I'll ever know. Like a lot of other 'Pilgrims,' though, Jake when first told of RMO's thought them to be a fresh water variety of the Malpeque. But, I'm getting ahead of myself here.

A couple of days after I arrived, Jake and I took off on a road trip. Over the course of several days we planned to contact 'customers' who had been supplying Jake and other investigators with illegal wildlife. Our first stop would be at a little cowboy bar about forty miles north of 'Old Mexico.' As luck would have it, we ran into a couple of Jake's 'customers' just as we pulled off of I-10. Transactions of the type we dealt with are rarely cut and dried. The preliminary wheeling and dealing occupied the time it took to shoot six or seven games of pool at this desert oasis. Bill, one of Jake's customers, asked us after the first round of negotiations, what our dinner plans were. Being thirty plus miles from the nearest establishment that required reservations, Jake said we were open. At this point Bill suggested we join him for "huevos" served out of doors at a local farm workers' village. Now some readers will recognize "huevos" as the Spanish term for eggs. In another context it also refers to the 'two items' a bull must part with to become a steer. In the interest of "furthering the investigation" we accepted Bill's invitation. Jake and I both hummed the tune from "I Wish I Were Any Place But Here" as we drove the eight or so miles to dinner. Once committed, neither of us could figure out a way to gracefully avoid dinner with out offending our 'customer'!

We arrived after dark. Bill introduced us around, and we continued our negotiations while our new found friends who spoke little English prepared dinner. Armloads of firewood carried to a central location constituted the kitchen area. After getting a fire built, one fella came into the firelight toting what I can only describe as a 'Rube Goldberg Wok'! This particular cooking apparatus had started out as one blade of a range land disc. After fulfilling that roll for who knows how long, it had been retired. Someone first welded the bolt holes shut, then found a piece of steel pipe the same diameter and welded a three inch side wall on the outside edge. With three metal legs welded on, it looked like a milking stool from Hell. Though not much to look at, this 'three legged wok' did appear to be functional.

To digress a little, let's go back to the town in Idaho that has the "World's Largest RMO Feed." The folks who put on this particular event, convert their bulls to steers at 2-3 months of age. At this age, the RMO's are about the size of the 'jawbreakers' we bought for a penny as kids. After being split, cleaned, breaded, deep fried to a crispy golden brown, and smothered in ketchup or salsa; they are served. It was this vision in my mind that kept telling my subconscious it would not be as bad as I anticipated.

Wrong!!! The cook started by pulling out a bucket of grease. I first thought, when I peeked into the bucket, that this must be a family heirloom for it looked so old. The cook's helper then showed up with a pail of large RMO's! And I mean large! Judging from their size, I estimated that the bulls who sacrificed these 'jewels of the pasture' to be 18-24 months old. We're not talking 'quail egg' size RMO's, we're talking about 'muy grande' size RMO's. Texas size if you will. But, I'm not sure what was bigger, the RMO's or Jake's and my eyes. Being a game warden requires a certain amount of machismo, which I'm sure contributed to our not chickening out and heading home before supper.

As the grease began heating, Jake and I fortified ourselves with several 12 oz. hydraulic sandwiches. Imagine eating a deep fried chunk of s@#%, the size of a hot dog bun with the texture of a pencil eraser! It took lots of beer and lots of hot salsa for me to eat with enough gusto to convince the cooks that I thoroughly enjoyed their cookin'!

At the risk of offending those whose mouths water as they read this story I must admit, I literally had to choke down my dinner!

I'm sure Jake and I weren't the first UC investigators to make a great personal sacrifice to 'further an investigation' but many years later it still sticks out in my mind, as well as in my throat. Jake later told me he always made sure to eat a big meal before stopping to see Bill and was damn glad when the investigation finally concluded!

Artichoke Chicken
—(Middle Fork "Choked" Chicken)—

Ingredients:

6 chicken breasts
Butter or margarine
12-24 oz. marinated artichoke hearts
1 4 oz. can mushrooms
½ cup chopped onion
1/3 cup all purpose flour
1 Tbsp. rosemary
Pinch of salt
1 can chicken broth
Wine

Brown chicken in butter or margarine and place in another Dutch oven. Cover chicken with artichokes and mushrooms. Saute onion in pan juices. Add flour, rosemary, salt, and pepper. Add broth and wine. Cook until bubbly. Spoon over chicken and cook for about an hour using 6-8 briquets for the bottom and 14-16 on the lid. Pour the remaining wine into cook.

Mark Armbruster
Idaho Fish & Game
Challis, Idaho

Baked Trout

Ingredients:

1-3 lb. trout
¼ cup melted butter or margarine
2 tsp. salt, 1 tsp paprika
Pinch of pepper
Dash of garlic powder
2 tsp. minced parsley
1 tsp. celery seed

Clean trout, removing head and tail. Split trout up back, leaving skin intact. Place skin side down in greased Dutch oven or baking pan. Combine butter or margarine, salt, paprika, pepper, and garlic powder. Brush over fish. Sprinkle with minced parsley. Bake for 20-30 minutes depending on the size of the trout. If at home, bake at about 425 degrees, or using 4-5 briquets underneath the Dutch and 20-22 briquets on the lid. Baste often with sauce. Fish will be flaky and moist when done. Garnish with celery seed.

Chicken Broccoli Divan

Ingredients:

4 cups chicken chunks, or turkey, or
            1 boned, cooked chicken
1 large bag frozen broccoli
2 cans cream of broccoli soup
2/3 cup milk
1 cup shredded cheddar cheese
Dab of margarine or butter
Breadcrumbs
Spices to taste – pepper, garlic, etc.

Combine thawed broccoli and chicken. Layer one-half broccoli/chicken mixture, putting one-third cheese on top. Cover with 1/3 cup milk mixed with 1 can of soup and spices. Repeat the broccoli/chicken layer topped with one-third of cheese. Cover with mixture of 1/3 cup milk, second can of soup, and spices. Add the rest of the cheese. Sprinkle breadcrumbs on top and dot with margarine or butter. Bake until bubbling.

Dan Miller
Steamboat Springs, Colorado

"No Class" enjoying a shower at Cougar Ranch
C.W. Welch Photo

——————— Beer Butt Chicken ———————

I've gathered recipes for this book from various sources and folks over the years. However, this anonymous contribution found its way to my mailbox and though it wouldn't fit in a Dutch oven, I wanted to include it in this book.

Ingredients:

1 whole chicken
1 Tbsp. season salt
1 Tbsp. garlic salt
1 can beer

Wash chicken inside and out. Drain well. Pat dry with paper towels. Combine season and garlic salts. Rub one-half of mixture on outside of chicken. Open the beer—drink one-third of it. Add remaining seasonings to rest of beer in the can (salt will bubble up—hold over sink). Place beer can in center of baking pan and as the name implies, set the chicken upright over the can of beer. Bake at 325 degrees for two hours or until done.

Chicken Gravy-Smothered
Chicken

Ingredients:

1 chicken, cut up
1 green bell pepper, cut up
1 onion, chopped
Salt/pepper
Flour
Water
1 can cream of chicken soup

Season the chicken with salt and pepper. Roll in flour. Place in a baking dish, adding some water for liquid. Cook for oven at 350 degrees for 30 minutes, covered. Add the cream of chicken soup and continue to cook uncovered for another 30 minutes. Serve with potatoes, rice, dumplings, biscuits, or cornbread.

Marie Mathis
Somerville, Texas

Chicken Parmesan

Ingredients:

1 chicken, cut up and skinned
1 small can Parmesan cheese
½ lb. butter, melted
Paprika/garlic powder/pepper

Dip chicken pieces in melted butter and coat with Parmesan cheese. Place coated chicken in Dutch oven and sprinkle with remaining cheese and spices. Bake until chicken is cooked, probably a little over an hour.

Cindy and John Thomas of Grand Junction, Colorado, shared this quick main dish on a trip down the Middle Fork of Salmon River in 1991.

—— Chicken Enchilada Casserole ——

Ingredients:

1 ½ lbs. chicken, diced
2 15 oz. cans green pork chili
1 11 oz. can cream of chicken soup
1 4 oz. can diced green chiles
1 4 oz. can mushroom pieces
1 onion, chopped
1 cup picante sauce
Spices – garlic powder, red pepper, cumin,
        paprika, chili powder
2 doz. corn tortillas, yellow or blue
1 lb. cheddar cheese, grated or shredded
8 oz. sour cream
1 jar picante salsa, chunky

Mix all ingredients above together, except tortillas, cheese, sour cream, and picante salsa, to form a thick sauce. Using a greased 12" Dutch oven, place layer of sauce, layer of grated cheddar cheese, layer of tortillas, layer of sauce, layer of cheese, layer of tortillas, etc., ending with layer of sauce and cheese on top. Sprinkle top with chili powder. Place 8-10 briquets under the Dutch oven and 14-16 briquets on the lid. Rotate Dutch oven and top occasionally to avoid any hot spots. Bake until casserole is bubbly, approximately 1 hour and 10 minutes. Serve with toppings of sour cream and picante salsa. This recipe can be made at home by baking at 350 degrees for approximately one hour. Cream of celery soup and chopped celery can be substituted for the cream of chicken soup and chopped onion.

Dan Miller
Tom Beck
Sandy Rost
Middle Fork of Salmon River, 1987

Three of my river pards first fixed this recipe on a 1987 Middle Fork trip. See "Religious Bedroll" for more details of that trip.

Chicken Gumbo

Ingredients:

2 lbs. chicken breasts cut into 1" chunks
2 tsp. dry mustard
2 tsp. paprika
¼ tsp. salt
¼ tsp. pepper
1/8 tsp. allspice
Pinch of cayenne pepper
2 Tbsp. olive oil
4 ribs celery, diced, ½ inch pieces
1 onion, coarsely chopped
1 red bell pepper, diced, ½ inch pieces
1 green bell pepper, diced, ½ inch pieces
4 cups okra
1 28 oz. can canned tomatoes, drained,
        saving the juice
2 Tbsp. tomato paste
1 tsp. thyme
1 bay leaf
¼ cup chopped parsley
1 Tbsp. crushed garlic

Rinse chicken and pat dry. Combine first 6 seasonings in a bowl and rub into chicken pieces. Lightly brown chicken and set aside. Place oil in Dutch oven. Add celery, onions, red and green peppers, and garlic. Stir and cook for 10 minutes. Add okra and cook additional 5 minutes. Add tomatoes, paste, thyme, bay leaf, chicken and pan juices to Dutch oven. Cover with saved tomato juice and parsley. Cook 1 hour. Serve over rice.

Mark Armbruster
Idaho Fish & Game
Challis, Idaho

Fish Casserole

Ingredients:

3 cups cooked pasta
2 cups cooked fish, such as halibut or salmon
2 cups mild, evaporated milk, or half & half
2 Tbsp. butter or margarine, melted
Salt/pepper/ seasonings
1/2 cup buttered bread crumbs

Drain and flake fish, removing any bones. Mix pasta, fish, milk, butter, and seasonings in a large bowl. Spoon mixture into a Dutch oven. Sprinkle buttered bread crumbs over the top. Bake for about an hour using 5-6 briquets under the oven and 20-25 briquets on the lid. Serves 6-8.

I came up with this recipe to utilize leftovers when we were filming our PBS series, *Dutch Oven and Camp Cooking*. To add a little extra zest, sprinkle with one-quarter cup seasoned rice vinegar before baking.

Hells Canyon Chukar

Ingredients:

4 chukars
Olive oil
Wild game seasoning
1 ½-2 cups white wine, chicken stock, or water
8-10 Juniper berries, optional

Place cleaned chukars in a 12" Dutch oven. Rub with olive oil and season to taste. Add the white wine, stock, or water. If there is a Juniper tree anywhere close, throw in the Juniper berries after you wash them. Cook with 6-8 briquets on the bottom and 16-20 briquets on the lid for about an hour. Serve with a side of wild rice, some steamed baby carrots, and a chunk of crusty bread. Serves 4.

D I S C O
(D'#$%'ed Incredible Stuff of Chicken
—————— for the Oven) ——————

Ingredients:

3 lbs. chicken breasts
1 lb. grated Swiss cheese
Enough pepper
1 can cream of chicken soup
¼ cup white wine
2 cups seasoned stuffing mix
¼ cup butter, melted
Parsley

Place breasts in bottom of Dutch oven. Cover with cheese and pepper. Mix soup and wine; then pour over the chicken. Cover with stuffing mix. Dribble with butter and sprinkle with parsley. Bake for 40-50 minutes, using 6-8 briquets on bottom and 14-16 on top. Put rest of wine in the chef.

Mark Armbruster
Idaho Fish & Game
Challis, Idaho

—————— Crabby Chicken ——————

Ingredients:

2-3 lbs chicken breasts, skinned
            (can use chukars, too)
1 pkg. imitation crab
2 packages white gravy mix
1 cup white wine
Salt, pepper, and garlic to taste
1 lb. sliced Swiss cheese

Prepare white gravy mixes according to package directions. Set aside. Fill your Dutch oven with the chicken and add the crab. Add the gravy over the meat in the Dutch. Add the white wine and seasonings. Cover the Dutch, bake with 6-8 briquets under the Dutch and 16-18 on the lid for about an hour. Cook until your crew is starving. It will get raving reviews one way or the other, but as my good friend, outfitter Jerry Myers, once said, "Hungair' es zee best sauce!" Add a thick layer of Swiss cheese, allow to melt and serve.

Tony Latham
Idaho Fish & Game
North Fork, Idaho

—————— Dutch Oven Halibut ——————

Ingredients:

4-5 lbs. halibut, cut into chunks, or fillets
3 Tbsp. olive oil
6-8 cloves garlic
4 Tbsp. fresh tarragon, chopped
1/4 cup lemon juice
2 cups white wine, or cooking liquid

Heat olive oil in 12" Dutch oven. Add garlic and saute for a few minutes, stirring constantly. Add fresh tarragon, lemon juice, and white wine or cooking liquid. Stir to blend all ingredients. Add halibut chunks or fillets, mix to coat the halibut with all the flavors. Cover and put Dutch oven into firepan. Put 6-8 briquets under the Dutch oven and 15 briquets on the lid. Cook 20-30 minutes depending upon the size of the chunks or fillets. When done, take off fire and remove halibut. Serve the juice as a sauce to be poured over halibut, or as an excellent dip for bread.

CAMP ROBBERS

Every once in awhile we find ourselves in a predicament which good sense tells us never to reveal, yet it's so good it can't be kept a secret! Since the statute of limitations has since expired, it's now safe to put this story in print!

The name *Perisoreus canadensis* probably doesn't ring a bell with most folks unless they happen to be an ornithologist by trade. However, anyone who has spent time in the Rocky Mountains may know this critter by one of its common names, Gray Jay, Canada Jay, Oregon Jay, or 'Camp Robber.' This denizen of the backwoods looks like an overgrown chickadee. As the name implies, it's gray in color. (Take note - the shade of gray matches exactly the gray in my old uniform shirts!) Although this particular bird is known as a camp robber, that function is practiced by many other critters. Anyone who camps, myself included, from time to time receives all sorts of unwanted visitors. Bears, crows, dogs, chipmunks, mice…porcupines will all drop into camp uninvited to partake of whatever they can eat or carry off. Of all the critters who do camp robbing, the Gray Jay exhibits a little more personality than the others. I've seen them swoop down, perch on a limb and just survey the scene. If they don't get anything to eat it doesn't seem to upset them at all. But, so much for the feathered and four legged camp robbers.

Memorial Day Weekend traditionally marks the opening of the general fishing season in Idaho. While most of the general populace heads to the hills for some R & R, game wardens head to work leaving their families to spend the long weekend by themselves. As opening day approached in 1996, I was preparing to transfer to another patrol area. My boss, Brent Hyde, who by the way has since been promoted to Assistant Chief of Enforcement, sent out a memo with work assignments for the holiday weekend. It came as no surprise to see my name paired with Brent's. According to the memo we would patrol the area streams with most of the guys detailed to different lakes and reservoirs. (Take note - Brent **was** the ranking member of this patrol!)

I packed a cooler with some sandwich stuff and sodas (for myself) before I left for Emmett to pick up Brent Saturday morning. I asked Brent if he was taking a lunch, and he said, "No!" The 'cricks' were swollen with spring runoff and consequently we encountered few fishermen that morning. Knowing it to be the last time we would likely work together in the field, we cruised the back roads, reminisced, and just enjoyed being out on a beautiful spring day! Brent is older than me, but close enough we ended up in college together. Brent hired on four years ahead of me and at that time had been my supervisor for five years. (Take note - based on both age and work experience, Brent was the most **senior** member of this patrol!)

As lunch approached Brent suggested I drive over to a small reservoir where Dan, Charlie, and Tom were working in plain clothes. Dan and Tom had spent the previous night camped above the lake and Charlie had joined them that morning. When we got in the area **Brent called** Tom on the radio and inquired about their lunch plans. Tom said they would head for camp once they finished making some contacts and for us to meet them there. Since Brent had previously assigned Tom to purchase 'camp groceries,' it was obvious to me Brent also planned to help them eat their grub. Tom made special mention that their camp was **not** where we normally camped. The only admission I will make is that I stopped the truck at a place that fit the description Tom gave us.

I gathered my lunch fixin's from my cooler and walked up to the camp with Brent. I offered to make him a sandwich but he declined saying he would see what Tom and Dan had. When we got to the camp it was obviously occupied by two people. There were two pair of shoes sitting next to the campfire, two sleeping bags in the blue tent Tom had described, and two lawn chairs. While I borrowed a knife to put mayo on my sandwich, Brent began rifling through the coolers. And as a supervisor Brent is always mindful of what his guys spend on groceries and gear. If my memory serves me correctly, Brent said something like, "I told those guys to go light on groceries, but they didn't have to go this light!"

Brent munched a few cookies and chips while he made a peanut butter sandwich with what little they had left. While watching Brent polish off all the groceries in sight, an eerie feeling came over me. The more I looked around the camp, I began to see things that didn't fit. Something wasn't right!

Tom and Dan are good friends, but not so good that they would share a twin size air mattress. Or at least I didn't think so. I reported my concerns to my supervisor like any conscientious employee would do. Brent laughed and pointed to the two pair of shoes and said, "Look at the shoes. Dan has big feet and Tom has small ones. This is their camp." I want to go on record here by saying I didn't agree with him! When I saw two lanterns, I knew for sure we were in the wrong place, and that Brent was eating someone else's grub! (Take note - Dan and Tom come to my deer camp every year.) I pointed to the lanterns and told Brent, "I've borrowed Tom's lantern and Dan doesn't have one!" Brent wasn't laughing now when he asked, "Are you serious?" I didn't have yes out of my mouth when Brent began hotfooting it for the truck!

We quickly got in the truck and drove up the road about a quarter mile. Our worst fears were realized when Tom, Dan, and Charlie passed and waved for us to follow them. At this point Brent, between bouts of uncontrollable laughter, said it was my fault for stopping where I did. I, of course, pointed out that as the **ranking senior more experienced** officer he should have pointed out my mistake earlier! When we did get to the other officers' camp, Brent had to admit that both camps appeared similar. Tom, Dan and Charlie were perplexed as to why every time Brent and I looked at each other, we burst into maniacal laughter. Later that afternoon as we headed for home, a pickup was parked in the 'other' camp. For all we knew these two folks had bushel baskets full of fish, but we weren't about to stop and check them.

We swore each other to secrecy, but it only lasted about two weeks. Brent started by telling his brother and I told my roommate. The rest is history because I can't think of four people in the world who could or would keep a secret like this one! My guess is the couple in that camp will someday read this story and it will put their minds at ease to know how and why they came back to camp only to find they had been robbed!

WANTED
For Camp Robbing

Brent Hyde
IDFG320

Consider Armed
with Hunger

—— River Sand Seafood Casserole ——

Ingredients:

4 Tbsp. green pepper
2 Tbsp. green onion
1 cup celery
1 cup crab meat
1 cup cooked shrimp
1 cup cooked rice
1 10 oz. pkg. frozen peas
½ tsp. Worchestershire sauce
½ tsp. pepper
1 cup mayonnaise
Crushed potato chips

Combine all ingredients except potato chips. Cover with chips and cook for 30 minutes. Add sand to taste!

Mark Armbruster
Challis, Idaho

———— Pheasant Stroganoff————

Ingredients:

3 pheasant breasts, cut into small pieces
        and dipped in flour
½ cup butter
½ cup chopped onion
1 cup chopped or sliced mushrooms
1 can mushroom soup
1 cup water
½ cup sour cream
Seasonings

Brown meat in butter in a Dutch oven. Season, add onions and mushrooms, and continue to brown. Add soup and water. Cover and simmer for about 20-30 minutes until thickened, using 6-8 briquets under the Dutch oven and 16-18 on the lid. Add sour cream, heat and serve over buttered noodles.

Cee Dub & Howard Konetzke fishing at Rockport, Texas
C.W. Welch Photo Collection

Fish Quiche

Ingredients:

1 cup shredded sharp cheddar cheese
2 cups cooked fish
1 Tbsp. flour
2 Tbsp. butter
1 bunch green onions, sliced, using 2" of the tops
1 can undiluted cream of mushroom soup
1 tsp. dill weed, not seed
2 eggs slightly beaten
1 unbaked 9-10" pie shell

Sprinkle half of cheese in pie shell. Mix fish with flour and place in shell. Saute onions in butter until soft, then add soup, sour cream, dill weed and pepper. Heat until near boiling, remove from heat, stir in eggs, and pour over fish. Sprinkle remaining cheese on top. At home bake at 325 degrees for 30 minutes or until set. Let stand for 10 minutes before serving. Very good with catfish, bass, or other warm water fish. Can be used even with trout, salmon, or canned tuna.

Herb Pollard

I make this in camp with a store-bought, ready-made pie crust. I set the pie plate on a small cake rack and use 6-8 briquets underneath the Dutch oven and 18-22 briquets on the lid.

Some-Like-It-Hot
—— Mexican Chukar Lasagna ——

This recipe was invented during a rigorous chukar hunt near Brownlee Reservoir.

Ingredients:

1 pkg. corn tortillas
1 can corn
4 medium fresh tomatoes, sliced or diced
3-4 jalapeno peppers (the chicken's way out),or
       3-4 fresh serrano peppers (the hero's way)
3 cloves garlic
1 16 oz. can of olives
1 19 oz. can of Hot Las Palmas Enchilada Sauce®
1 lb. Monterey Jack cheese, shredded
1 lb. cheddar, shred
2 chukars, diced

Cook in a 12" Dutch oven. Layer in a Dutch oven alternating all of the ingredients until 2 inches from the top. Sprinkle a light layer of cheese on the top. Use 6 briquets on the bottom and 10 on top, and cook for 1 hour. Add 5-6 briquets on top the last 10-15 minutes to weld.

Robert Stauts
Boise, Idaho

Spruce Grouse and
—————— Pasta for One ——————

Ingredients:

1 spruce grouse, cleaned
1-2 Tbsp. olive oil
1-2 cans of beer
1 cup pasta
1-2 cups water
¼ cup ranch dressing

Cut grouse into serving pieces and brown in the olive oil. Pour one can of beer over the grouse, cover, and let simmer for quite a while. If the beer simmers away, check the grouse for doneness by gnawing on a drum stick. If it is still tough, add the other beer and let simmer for a while longer. Add the pasta and water. Cook until the pasta is done. Toss in the ranch dressing and serve.

———— Seafood Florentine Bake ————

Ingredients:

2 lbs. fish fillets – flounder, haddock, pollock, etc.
1 tsp. salt
½ tsp. onion powder
½ tsp. pepper
1 can condensed cream of shrimp
         or cheddar cheese soup
1 10 oz. pkg. chopped spinach,
         thawed and well drained
2 cups Bisquick® baking mix, or equivalent
1/3 cup grated Parmesan cheese
1 cup milk
2 eggs

Heat oven to 350 degrees or preheat a Dutch oven. Arrange fish in greased pan or in the Dutch with a coating of oil on the bottom. Add salt, pepper, and onion powder to taste. Spoon soup over fillets and top with spinach. Beat remaining ingredients and pour over spinach. Bake for about 50 minutes. If using a regular oven, bake uncovered. Serves 8.

Mile McLain
Colorado Division of Wildlife
Middle Fork, 1992

COOKIN' with KRAUT

Marriage changes everyone who says, "I DO"! Few will argue that these changes do not occur, and in all honesty one must agree that change is good! (Sometimes though it takes a while to see the Good.) For we men, these changes run the gamut from putting the seat back down to wearing color-coordinated clothes. Somewhere on the list, food choices show up sooner or later. Like a balky mule, some menu items cause the changee to curl his lip and others cause him to wonder why it took so long to make the change. Much to my wife's relief, sauerkraut fell into the later category!

Years ago Mom would fix sauerkraut and wieners for us kids. It was a quick fix when she got home from work late. Few things were simpler! Slice up a package of wieners and throw them in a pot with a couple of cans of store-bought kraut and dinner was done. While a game warden, I'd throw a couple of cans of kraut and some pre-cooked sausages in my chuck box as a backup meal in case a trip extended longer than planned. Until I met my wife, kraut fell into the lowest 20% of foods I liked. It was palatable and would do in a pinch.

Being Czech, she started eating kraut as soon as she quit taking her food through a nipple. By the time we met, she held an advanced degree in judging the quality of kraut and how to cook it! From her I learned the sour in sauerkraut doesn't have to be overpowering. If using store-bought kraut, she prefers fresh over the canned. First thing, she pours it into a colander and rinses it two or three times with warm water. Much of the sour taste ends up going down the drain. Kraut prepared after rinsing takes on the seasoning of the dish being prepared without an overpowering 'sour' taste.

Store-bought kraut is a thing of the past around our house now though! Last year a neighbor taught us an anaerobic method of making homemade kraut with no muss, no fuss, no foul odors, and no skimming of scum. It seems that no matter how many quarts we put up, they disappear in just a short time. Whether planning a meal at home or a menu for a camping trip, I've changed the rating on kraut to the top 20%!

── Roast Goose with Sauerkraut ──

Ingredients:

6-8 lb. goose, or duck
Salad or vegetable oil
Salt/pepper/seasonings
2 medium onions, or peeled apples
2-3 cans or packages of sauerkraut,
       drained and liquid saved
Caraway seed

Rinse goose or duck thoroughly and pat dry. Rub salad or vegetable oil on the goose to coat. Season the bird to taste. Put onions or apples in the body cavity to cook with the bird. Place bird on a rack in a deep 14" Dutch oven. Sprinkle caraway seed on the outside of the bird. Add liquid previously drained and reserved from sauerkraut to cook bird. Cover and place Dutch oven in firepan. Cook with 8-10 briquets underneath and 20-25 briquets on top for about 1 hour. Add sauerkraut over and around the bird. Continue to cook until brown and getting tender. Freshen charcoal as needed.

Two whole mallard ducks will just fit inside a deep 12" Dutch oven if you don't have a deep 14" DO.

──── Words of Wisdom ────
When using cast iron cookware be careful not to scrape dried food residue too vigorously with metal spoons and spatulas. If you scratch through the protective coating of the cure you will end up with sticky spots.

Roast Turkey & Dressing

Ingredients:

12-13 lb. turkey, halved through the breast,
  using only half, and freezing the other
  half for another dinner
Small amount of salad oil
Salt/pepper/poultry seasonings
2 cups chicken broth, dry white wine, water

Wash the turkey half and pat dry. Rub the bird with salad oil and season with salt, pepper, and favorite poultry seasonings. Place the turkey on a rack breast side up in a 14" deep Dutch oven. Add broth, wine, or water for cooking liquid. Put the lid on the DO and place in firepan. Cook with 8-10 briquets underneath and 20-25 briquets on top for about 1-1 1/2 hours or until starting to brown and get tender. Freshen charcoal as needed. Add the dressing by spooning around the bird in the Dutch oven. Add additional liquid, if necessary. Cover, add fresh charcoal and continue to cook for about 45 minutes and serve.

Dressing Ingredients:

10-12 cups stale or toasted bread and
  onion bagels, cubed
4-5 ribs celery cut into 1" pieces
1 can black olives, sliced
2 medium yellow onions, diced
3-4 cups stock with giblets, spiced with peppercorns,
  bay leaves, sage, oregano, and thyme
1/2 stick butter

Mix dry ingredients in a large bowl. Cook giblets in water spiced with peppercorns or ground pepper, bay leaves, sage, thyme, and oregano. Pull the giblets out of the stock and let cool. Dice cooked and cooled giblets and add to dry ingredients. Add butter to stock and bring to a boil. Pour over the dry ingredients and stir to moisten thoroughly. Spoon around bird and cook as described above.

MESQUITE ROAST WILD TURKEY

After bagging a wild turkey, I wet pick, clean, and freeze it whole with the giblets and neck tucked inside the carcass in a separate bag.

Since wild turkeys are built a little different that the vacuum-packed, store-bought variety, it takes a little extra work to fit one in a Dutch oven. I separate the hindquarters from the rest of the turkey, and then split them down the backbone. At this point I take a fillet knife and disjoint each leg from the backbone, getting as much meat off the backbone as I can. I cook the leg in one piece, but you can disjoint at the thigh if you choose. To remove the ribs from the front half of the bird, cut along each side of the backbone and work your knife along the outside of the ribs down each side to where they attach to the breast bone and grasping the neck pull backward. Save the two back pieces.

After getting your bird cut up, put the giblets, neck, and back pieces to boil in a pot with 2 quarts water and season to taste. Dice up a medium onion and add to the broth. I like to add a couple of bay leaves and a pinch each of sage, oregano, and thyme. Wipe the turkey drumsticks and the breast with olive oil and season with cracked pepper or seasonings of your choice. I start 8-10 charcoal briquets in my Weber® grill. When they are ready, I scoot them to one side of the grill and place 2-3 chunks of mesquite wood on them. Once the mesquite starts smoking, I lay the breast and drumsticks on the opposite side of the grill. The intent is to flavor the meat and not cook it with direct heat. Let it smoke for no more than 15-20 minutes or it will dry out.

Transfer the turkey to a deep 14" Dutch oven with a rack in the bottom. Take 2 cups of the broth from the pot the giblets are boiling in for a cooking liquid. Roast for 1 ½-2 hours with 6-8 briquets underneath the Dutch and 16-18 on the lid. Make dressing and gravy with the broth. Add dressing to the turkey pieces about 50 minutes before serving.

"Gobble, Gobble"   C.W. Welch Photo

———— Goose and Noodles ————

Next time you roast a goose for dinner, don't cover the
leftovers and put them in the refrigerator. Roast goose, in
my experience, gets tough and dry even if it's well wrapped.
After dinner put the carcass in a large stockpot with about a
gallon of water, set it on the stove and simmer until the
meat falls off the bones. Usually this takes only a couple of
hours. Let cool and pull all remaining meat off the carcass.
Discard bones and skin. Refrigerate if you're going to make
this in the next day or two, or freeze it for later use. I prefer
to freeze the meat with about two quarts of the broth. For a
quick camp dinner, I pull the broth out of the cooler in the
morning and allow it to thaw. That evening just pour it in a
pot and add a pound of egg noodles after the broth comes
to a boil. In about ten minutes you have a delicious and
nutritious main dish. Serve with coleslaw and hard rolls.

Vicki's Deep-Fried Chicken

Ingredients:

1 chicken, cut into pieces
Ice water and ice cubes
1/4-1/3 cup salt
1 Tbsp. pepper
1 cup flour

Place chicken in a large bowl and cover with ice water. Add salt to ice water and mix together until salt is dissolved. Add more ice as needed. Chill in refrigerator overnight for best flavor. If in a hurry, chill at least for a couple of hours. The longer, the better. Heat oil in deep frying pan. Mix pepper with flour. Put flour mixture in a paper bag or large plastic bag. Coat chicken with flour by placing a couple of pieces of chicken at a time in the bag and shaking. Place flour-coated chicken in the hot oil to fry. Turn frequently to brown evenly. When the chicken pieces float to the top of the oil and are thoroughly brown, they are done.

Vicki Konetzke
Katy, Texas

Cee Dub & Sis take it easy in camp
Penny Welch Photo

——— Sage Grouse Supreme ———

Fillet and cut 2 sage grouse into 1" cubes. Soak in milk for several hours or overnight. Drain and pat dry. Coat with seasoned flour (to flour add generous amounts of paprika, garlic salt, onion salt, and pepper—flour should have a red tint). Brown in hot oil. Place in Dutch oven and add:

Ingredients:

1 cup brewed coffee
1 15 oz. can tomato sauce
3 Tbsp. grape jelly
1 cup red wine
1 4 oz. can mushrooms, drained

Cover and cook using 8-10 briquets underneath the Dutch oven and 15-18 briquets on the lid, or in a 350 degree oven. For adult birds, which may be tough, plan on cooking about 2 ½ hours. You'll need to freshen your charcoal for the last hour. Check periodically and add more wine or water if needed. Serve with rice or noodles and a green salad. Serves four. This is a good recipe for old as well as young birds. Pheasant can be substituted for sage grouse.

When I first went to work for Idaho Fish and Game as a "Bio-Logical" Aide, I worked for Bob Autenrieth on "The Sage Grouse Study." Besides gaining three summers of valuable field experience, Bob passed on a couple of his recipes. This one is great, and don't let the unorthodox ingredients fool you!

——— Roast Wild Goose ———

Take one cleaned goose and rub the cavity with salt, and place several pats of butter or margarine in cavity. Fill cavity with carrots, potatoes, apples and orange. Place goose on rack in a roasting pan or 14 " Dutch oven and cook in a slow oven or with 8-10 briquets under the Dutch oven and 20-25 briquets on the lid. Baste every 10 minutes with the following sauce:

Ingredients:

4 cloves garlic, crushed
1 Tbsp. parsley
2 cups dry white wine
½ cube butter
½ tsp. Italian herbs
1 Tbsp. apple cider vinegar
Salt and pepper to taste

 ——————— Words of Wisdom ——
Keep a can handy to pour excess fat into. Don't pour it in the fire ring or out on the ground.

——— Marie's Fried Chicken ———

Ingredients:

1 5 lb. chicken, cut up
Salt/pepper
Pinch of seasoning salt
Pinch of garlic powder

Season the chicken with the spices. Cover and refrigerate for four hours. Roll the chicken in flour. Fry for FOURTEEN minutes. Serve with baked potatoes and Marie's Green Beans.

Marie Mathis
Somerville, Texas

Marie is a "Cooks' Cook!" She's a walking encyclopedia of "Southern Cooking" at its best My wife and I met her at Round Top, Texas, while she was cooking for a friend of mine, Howard Konetzke, Jr. Howard owns the "Old Depot Antiques" in Round Top, the central location of two large community-based antique fairs each year. Marie takes time away from her regular cooking to cook in Howard's restaurant during the shows. She keeps the folks smiling, content, and coming back.

——Hells Canyon Salmon Steaks——

Ingredients:

4-6 Salmon steaks, cut ¾ " thick
2 tsp. dill weed
1-2 cups dry white wine

Put steaks in a 12" Dutch oven. Sprinkle dill on the Salmon steaks. Add the white wine. Put the D/O in the firepan with 8-10 briquets on the bottom and 12-14 briquets on top. Cook for about 15 minutes. Watch for steam coming from the D/O. Be careful not to overcook the Salmon.

8-10 cloves garlic, mashed or minced fine
2-3 Tbsp. butter or margarine
1/2 tsp. dill weed
Juice of one lemon

In a 10" Dutch oven, sauté the garlic in the butter. Add the dill weed and the juice. Simmer to reduce the liquid.

When steaks are almost done, garnish with the garlic, lemon, and dill sauce. Serve with French or garlic bread and Rainbow Rice.

Idaho's once bountiful Salmon runs have diminished greatly in the last 30+ years. As a result, sport fishing opportunities for this tastiest of salmon occur rather infrequently. With the future of the species in doubt, this dish was a treat for the soul as well when I fixed it for my son and friends, utilizing Brian's first salmon. The question we asked that night in Hells Canyon after supper, "Would his children ever get the same chance to catch and eat a Salmon from Idaho?"

———— Words of Wisdom ————

When possible scrub vegetables such as carrots, potato's, turnips, instead of peeling them. Many of the nutrients in veggies are next to the skin plus the peelings add considerably to your garbage load.

—— Rick's Quick Italian Chicken ——

Ingredients:

4 chicken breasts, pre-cooked (baked or BBQ'd),
       cut into small pieces ahead of time
1 pkg. favorite pasta or noodles
3 cups chicken bouillon or broth, optional
1 jar Alfredo sauce
       (Rick likes Five Brothers Mushroom Flavor™)
1 small can mushrooms

Cook the pasta or noodles on your camp stove according to package directions, using the bouillon or broth as part of the cooking liquid, if desired, to give the pasta a better flavor. Drain the pasta or noodles. Add the Alfredo sauce, olives, mushrooms, and chicken. Continue to heat until all ingredients are thoroughly heated up. That's It!

Rick Carrico
 Twin Falls, Idaho

═══ TWO RELUCTANT COOKS ═══

Someone once said that there are two kinds of people; leaders and followers! To paraphrase that from a camping perspective there are cooks and eaters! Every camp cook I've known started out as an eater, but somewhere along the way made the switch to camp cook! Rather than explore what motivates folks to become camp cooks, I'll take you on a journey with two friends who made the switch.

Along in the late '70's and early '80's, a group of us began running rivers in the West. The core of the group traced their roots to college days. With sheepskins in hand we had scattered all over the West and took jobs with resource management agencies. The nature of our work dictated we spend a fair amount of our time camping and being bachelors, (sometimes intermittently); there wasn't anyone around to do the cooking but ourselves. When we started running rivers, the cooking chores did not present any problems. As time went by the group grew larger. The new additions seemed in awe of the creations set before them each day by the cooks. It didn't take too long before this became a real drag for the one or two people cooking! A division of labor seemed in order.

Anyone who has cooked for a large group realizes the immensity of the challenge for a neophyte. To help these folks ease into the camp cooking world, we started by assigning them to do lunches. It's tough to mess up a lunch of cold cuts, gorp, and lemonade. Even then the responsibility of providing a meal that doesn't require any cooking for a large group will cause some consternation! Making the jump to a dinner meal tends to raise the anxiety level.

Jim Van Ark and Pat Weber joined the group as passengers/eaters, and by June, 1991 had graduated to running their own boat when we launched for a Grand Canyon trip on the Colorado River. In the jargon of river runners, 'pucker factor,' does not refer to something immediately preceding a kiss. A river running buddy of mine once defined it as…the greater the pucker factor, the more swings it takes with a four pound hammer to drive a straight pin into a spot you normally wouldn't try to place a pin! Of our group, only Tom Beck had ever floated this stretch of the Colorado. Fear of the unknown infected the rest of us. Each rapid produced episodes of anticipation and apprehension that contributed to the collective pucker power of the group. Though we didn't test the 'pucker factor' of individuals, my guess is that Jim and Pat would've showed up on such a list as either, "Win, Place, or Show."

Downloading of adrenaline commenced each afternoon when we pulled into our campsite! Though on the evenings Pat and Jim cooked, their download didn't start until after dinner. Somewhere below Granite Rapids their confidence caught up with their skills, both on the river and in the kitchen. My trip diary makes special mention of the clam linguini and upside down cake they served for dinner on Day #13.

——Van Weber's Clam Linguine——

Ingredients:

8 oz. uncooked linguine
1-2 Tbsp. olive oil
½ tsp. dried thyme
¼ tsp. crushed red pepper
½ cup chopped onion
1-2 cloves garlic, minced
2 6 oz. cans chopped clams, undrained
½ cup 2% milk
1 large egg
½ cup (2 oz.) grated fresh Parmesan cheese
1/3 cup chopped fresh parsley

Cook pasta according to directions, omitting salt and fat, and drain. While pasta cooks, heat oil in a large skillet over medium heat. Add thyme, red pepper, onion, and garlic. Cook until onion is golden brown, about 6 minutes. Stir in undrained clams and bring to boil. Add pasta to pan. Combine milk and egg in a small bowl, and stir well with a whisk. Add milk mixture to pan and stir well. Cook over low heat 5 minutes until milk mixture is thick, stirring constantly. Do not boil. Sprinkle mixture with cheese and parsley. Serve immediately. Yield is 4 servings of 1 cup each. Obviously one needs to expand for a hungry river crew, but it's quick and not every dish used like the author!!!!!!

Jim Van Ark
Pat Weber
Challis, Idaho

MEATS

SOMETHING SOFT FOR DINNER

If you like to eat, taking off on a back country trip with someone you don't know well who says he will do the cooking, presents the same chance for success as going on a blind date arranged by your sister. But...as an old boss of mine used to say, "Life is nothing but a series of missed opportunities!" You have to take the chance, but it's unwise to let your expectations get too high. Anyway...

In late August, 1983, my boss passed some information on to me about two fellas who had drawn permits to hunt bighorn sheep along Idaho's Middle Fork of Salmon River and were allowing two other guys to go hunting in their place. Such a transfer is, of course, contrary to Idaho Code. Al told me to put together an operation which if successful might educate these guys and generate a little income for the state judicial system at the same time. I enlisted Russ Kozacek and Paul Valcarce to help with the operation. The plan went something like this. Paul and I would fly a float boat into Indian Creek and float down to the mouth of Loon Creek and meet Russ with his pack string. Russ and Paul would head up toward Norton Ridge where our informant said these guys planned to hunt. I would set up surveillance on a trail junction should they miss the guys up on the mountain. Russ and I split picking up the camp groceries and cooking duties. I would take care of everything along the river, and Russ would provide for Paul and him while on horseback. No problem!?!?!

Russ readily admits that he and I come from different camp cooking schools. Russ graduated with honors from the school that teaches folks to fix the simplest, quickest recipes that result in the fewest dirty dishes. The ability to boil water is high on the list of criteria required to graduate from this particular school that shall remain un-named here! The grub in his camp isn't fancy but there is always enough. That is, until this trip.

At the appointed time we met at the US Forest Service tent frame located about a half mile below the confluence of Big Loon Creek with Middle Fork.

Let me digress here and tell you a little more about where we met. At this time the USFS stationed a person at the tent frame during the summer float season. The fireguard had pulled out just a week before we arrived. Among other duties, this person kept the one-hole outhouses located at float camps supplied with toilet paper. More than once I'd stopped to re-supply when my own stocks of this vital commodity ran low.

While Paul and I sorted his stuff, Russ started putting things in two different piles. One pile they would take with them on the trail, and another pile to leave with me at our base camp. Out of the corner of my eye I saw Russ pick up some of the "Woodsy Owl" drawstring garbage bags to stow stuff in out of the tent frame. Coincidentally, the fireguard kept his extra TP in the same bags hung on a nail next to the door. With all three of us working, it didn't take long to get the pack stock loaded. After agreeing on radio codes and check-in times, Russ and Paul pulled out.

I squared my gear around after they left, then pulled a paperback book out of my duffel and began the surveillance. I fixed a chicken and pasta dish in my 10" aluminum DO and sat on the porch maintaining surveillance as long as I had reading light. Then it came time to light a lantern and move inside. I reached into the "Woodsy Owl" bag for a roll of TP prior to taking a stroll up the hill to the privy. Only when we compared notes several days later did we determine that we'd made simultaneous discoveries! I reached in expecting to grab a soft round roll, not a foil wrapped package containing freeze-dried beef stroganoff! Meanwhile, up on Norton Ridge, Russ ended up being the one to grasp what I was looking for! Later, there was considerable confusion over WHO was responsible for the switch! In my case I substituted a copy of the previous year's fishing regulations for what I needed, while Russ and Paul split a can of kipper snacks and a couple of granola bars found at the bottom of a saddle bag.

If there is a moral to this story it's this. Even if you're not the cook, at least check to make sure the cook packs the grub!

Beef and Asparagus

Ingredients:

¼ lb. beef, sliced
1 lb. asparagus
½ cup soy sauce for marinating beef
1 Tbsp. soy sauce
Salt and pepper to taste
2 Tbsp. oil for stir-frying
1 clove garlic, minced

Marinate beef in soy sauce for 20-30 minutes. Slice asparagus diagonally into 1 ½ inch pieces.

Stir-fry beef in oil until cooked. Set aside. Stir-fry garlic in oil until slightly brown. Add asparagus and continue stir-frying until done. Asparagus should be crisp, not overcooked. Add the cooked beef and stir in the soy sauce, salt, and pepper until everything is well mixed. Remove and serve. Broccoli may be used if asparagus is not available.

Cheryl Bridges
Idaho Fish & Game
Boise, Idaho

A Dutch oven can be used as a wok if you have a camp stove which will let the legs of the Dutch oven sit through the grate. This is an easy and delicious stove top meal that will impress your campers.

Barbequed Beef Brisket

Ingredients:

4-5 lbs. beef brisket, trimmed
1 onion sliced to make rings
1 1/2-2 cups red wine or water
BBQ sauce

Beef Rub Ingredients:

2 Tbsp. sweet paprika
1 Tbsp garlic powder
1 Tbsp. black pepper, coarsely ground
1 Tbsp. dried thyme
1 Tbsp. dried basil
1 Tbsp. dried parsley

Combine all ingredients in a small bowl and mix well. Apply rub to meat, even the ends, and coat as thickly as possible. Place meat in a deep 14" Dutch oven on a rack, if possible. Add 1 1/2-2 cups of red wine or water as a cooking liquid. Place Dutch oven in firepan with 10-12 briquets on the bottom and 20 briquets on top. Cook for 2 hours, or until tender. This is a fairly tough cut of meat. It will likely be necessary to add new charcoal after 1 to 1 1/2 hours to complete cooking. Remove meat from DO when meat is done. Let it rest for 10 minutes before cutting. Slice and serve with BBQ sauce on the side. Served with coleslaw and cornbread, this makes a great meal in camp or at home on the patio.

———————— Pat's Beef Brisket ————————

Ingredients:

3-4 lbs beef brisket
1/3 cup vermouth
1 can cream of mushroom soup
1 pkg. onion soup mix

Mix ingredients together. Pour over brisket in Dutch oven. If you're at home, cook at 225 degrees for 5 hours, covered. This is a good dish for a lay over day on a river trip or for a camp day when the cook stays in camp. If in camp, use 6-8 briquets underneath the Dutch and 16 on top. Freshen charcoal every 1 ½ hours. Save a little vermouth to add if your cooking liquid needs refreshed. Or, if out of vermouth, use water. Makes good gravy. Serve with rice, noodles, or potatoes.

Pat Cudmore
Boise, Idaho

—— Blue Cheese Lamb Chops ——

Ingredients:

4 lamb chops
Crushed garlic
Salt
Pepper
2-3 Tbsp. heavy cream
Chunk of blue cheese

Season the chops with the crushed garlic, salt, and pepper. Place on a grill and cook until thoroughly brown. Turn over and cook other side. Mix the cream and blue cheese together to make a paste. When second side of chops are brown, turn back over on the grill. Spread the blue cheese paste on the chops and continue to cook until the paste melts into the meat. Then they're ready. Serve with a little mint jelly, baked potatoes, and a salad.

This recipe can be used with pork chops, too, and can be done in a Dutch oven rather than on a grill. If using lamb chops in the Dutch oven, the fat rendered from browning the chops can be drained off to enhance the flavor of the chops prior to applying the blue cheese paste.

Rick Carrico
Twin Falls, Idaho

———— Curried Venison————

Ingredients:

2 lbs. cubed venison, a tender cut
3 cloves garlic, minced
1 small onion, diced
1 Tbsp. curry powder
1 cup beef stock

Saute garlic in olive oil. Add venison and diced onion, and fry for 5-7 minutes. Add the beef stock and curry powder and simmer for 45 minutes. Serve over rice.

If you take pets to camp make sure to put food in for them as well. Don't plan on feeding them table scraps. Pack their food and water dishes also. Unless you've trained your dog to use an outhouse, pack a shovel and save others the chore of scrapping off the soles of their shoes!

Bob's Lasagna
——— The Long Way Around ———

This lasagna's not for the lazy cook, but for a lazy guy who's staying in camp instead of hunting, fishing, hiking…you get the picture.

Ingredients:

1 pkg. lasagna noodles
1 large onion
4 cloves garlic
3 fresh tomatoes or 1 large can chopped tomatoes
1 red bell pepper
1 green bell pepper
1 can tomato paste
3 hard boiled eggs
1 pint ricotta cheese
1 ½ lb. mozzarella cheese
8 oz. Romano cheese
4 oz. Parmesan cheese
2 hot Italian sausages
1 mild Italian sausage

Cook in a 12" Dutch oven. Saute all of the vegetables with the garlic in the Dutch until onions are clear. Remove from pan. Slice the sausages in small circles and brown in the same pan, then remove. In a saucepan, combine tomatoes, tomato paste and vegetables. Simmer for 30 minutes. Thin slice the hard boiled eggs. In a separate bowl, mix mozzarella, Romano, and ricotta cheese together. Leave the Parmesan for sprinkling separately later.

Using dry lasagna noodles, layer in the Dutch oven. Start first layer with approximately 1 cup of sauce. Then layer with noodles, meat, eggs, and cheese, alternating until filled 2 inches from the top of the Dutch. Sprinkle Parmesan on top and cover. Use 6 briquets under the Dutch, 10 on the lid, and cook for 1 hour. Add 5-6 briquets on top the last 10-15 minutes to weld.

Robert Stauts
Boise, Idaho

—— Dutch Chinese Casserole ——

Ingredients:

1 lb. hamburger
1 cup onions
1 cup celery
1 can cream of mushroom soup
1 can cream of chicken soup
¼ cup water
½ cup uncooked rice
¼ cup soy sauce
1 can bean sprouts, drained
1 can chow mein vegetables
1 can chow mein noodles

Brown meat and add stuff in order except dry noodles. Bake 1 hour. Last 15-20 minutes, add dry noodles.

Mark Armbruster
Idaho Fish & Game
Challis, Idaho

Dutch Oven Tamale Pie

Ingredients:

1-2 chopped onions
1 lb. ground beef
1 lb. pork sausage
1 teaspoon minced garlic
1 28 oz. can tomatoes
1 can corn
1 can olives
1 can Mexican tomato sauce
Enough chili powder to make it burn
Same with Cumin
Oregano
'Bout 20 small corn tortillas
½ lb. cheddar cheese, shredded

Brown onion, garlic, beef, and sausage. Add all the other stuff, except the tortillas and cheese, and cook a while. Put one-half of mixture in bottom of Dutch oven, about ½ inch deep. Cover with one-half the tortillas. Repeat layers. Bake about 30 minutes using 6-8 briquets on bottom and 14-16 briquets on top. Cover with cheese the last 5 minutes or so. Eat the stuff and get someone else to do the dishes.

Mark Armbruster
Idaho Fish & Game
Challis, Idaho

Pork Chops 'n' Kraut

Ingredients:

4 pork chops, lean and thick
1 quart sauerkraut
1 15 oz. can diced tomatoes
Salt/pepper/seasonings

Brown seasoned pork chops in a small amount of olive or vegetable oil. Place chops in baking dish or Dutch oven. Cover with sauerkraut and tomatoes. Bake at 350 degrees for one hour in the oven, or place covered Dutch oven on 4-6 briquets with 18-22 briquets on the lid for 50-60 minutes. Recipe can be doubled easily for a larger group.

Vicki Konetzke
Katy, Texas

——— Words of Wisdom ———

Treat wooden utensils with mineral oil before you head for camp. If your leaving wood utensils in your camp box over winter, give them a coat of oil when you put them away. At home, wash wooden utensils by hand and not in the dishwasher. The high heat dries them out.

——— Corned Beef & Cabbage ———

Ingredients:

3-4 lbs. corned beef brisket
6-8 red potatoes, washed
2 medium onions, quartered
4-6 carrots, cut into 1" chunks
3 celery stalks, cut into 1" chunks
1 head cabbage, cored and cut into wedges
Salt/pepper/seasonings
3-4 cups water

Trim off excess fat from corned beef. Boil with seasonings in a deep 14" Dutch oven for about 1 1/2 hours. Add vegetables and continue to boil until vegetables are nearly done, but still firm. Add cabbage and cook entire mixture until vegetables are tender.

Save any leftover corned beef for making sandwiches for lunch with rye bread and some sauerkraut, along with dill pickles. Try this with corned venison if you can. Our local butcher corns venison for us and it's delicious.

─── Easy Dutch Oven Lasagna ───

Ingredients:

1 lb. ground beef
1 onion, minced
1 ½ qts. cottage cheese
1 large pkg. lasagna noodles
1 large can tomato sauce
1 lb. mozzarella cheese
½ lb. mushrooms, sliced
Basil
Oregano
½ cup red wine

Cook lasagna noodles according to package directions. Brown beef and onion. Place ½ in bottom of Dutch oven. Add ½ each of cottage cheese, noodles, tomato sauce, basil, oregano, and wine. Repeat layers. Bake 30-35 minutes. Cover with Mozzarella cheese and mushrooms. Bake 10 minutes more.

Mark Armbruster
Idaho Fish & Game
Challis, Idaho

─── Ham and Noodle Casserole ───

Ingredients:

½ tsp. salt
6 oz. noodles
½ lb. ham, finely diced
½ lb. cheddar cheese, finely grated
1 green pepper, finely diced
2 Tbsp. chopped onion
1 can cream of mushroom soup
2/3 cup milk
1/3 cup melted butter
Buttered breadcrumbs or mashed corn flakes

Cook noodles in salted water. Mix all ingredients except breadcrumbs or corn flakes. Pour into a greased 12" Dutch oven. Cover and bake for 30-40 minutes at 350 degrees using 4-6 briquets under the Dutch oven and 18-20 briquets on the lid. Remove lid and sprinkle breadcrumbs or corn flakes on top. Bake until browned. Serves 6-8.

Butch radio-collaring elk on S. Fork Clearwater River Winter 1998
C.W. Welch Photo Collection

———————— Garden Pot Roast ————————

Ingredients:

> 1 leg of lamb, large beef pot roast, or elk roast
> 3-4 Tbsp. olive oil
> 5-6 cloves garlic, sliced
> 2 cups beef stock (red wine can also be used)
> 1/2 doz. boiling onions, or small onions
> 3-4 turnips, quartered
> 1/2 doz. small, red spuds
> 3-4 carrots, cut into 1" chunks
> 1 doz. brussels sprouts

In a deep 14" Dutch oven, or a roaster at home, sauté the garlic in the olive oil. Quickly brown the roast. Add the stock. Cook the roast for 1 ½ hours. Add more charcoal as needed. Add the veggies and cook for another hour or until vegetables are tender. Serve with a good loaf of bread.

Parmesan Pork Steak

Ingredients:

6-8 pork steaks
1/3 cup olive oil
6 cloves garlic, sliced
¾ cup Parmesan cheese
1 12 oz. can beer
Wild game seasoning

Heat olive oil in a 12" Dutch oven. Add the garlic. Brown the pork steaks in the olive oil and garlic. Layer in the Dutch oven, sprinkling each layer with Parmesan cheese. Season with the wild game seasoning. Add the beer, cover, and cook with 6-8 briquets under the oven and 20-22 on top. Bake for 40 minutes.

If you have leftovers, warm them up and serve with hash browns and eggs for a quick and hearty breakfast.

HANK'S SPAGHETTI SAUCE

If you search long enough you'll find an interesting story behind almost every recipe, some of them worth repeating. Sandy Riney of *Las Piedras Ranch* passed on the story of how her father, Colonel Henry G. Casey, came by this recipe during WWII. The then, Captain Casey, was flying supplies to Patton's Third Army from Naples, Italy. It seemed like every time Capt. Casey went to his favorite restaurant for pasta, air raid sirens interrupted his dinner. He was able to get next door to a bomb shelter with his martini, but not his pasta. Though I've never been in one, it's my guess you get fairly close to those you share a bomb shelter with. Anyway…in the course of sitting out an air raid, Hank made the acquaintance of the restaurant's proprietor. Over a couple of martinis that made it into the bomb shelter with Hank, he asked the restaurant owner for his spaghetti sauce recipe. Hank said that at the time a plate of pasta cost two bits!

——— Hank's Spaghetti Sauce ———

Ingredients:

1 lb. ground meat, brown and set aside
1 large onion, finely chopped
½ green bell pepper, finely chopped
1 clove garlic, minced
¼ cup olive oil
1 large can pureed tomatoes
2 cups water
1 bay leaf
Tabasco®, to taste
1 cup sliced mushrooms

Saute the onion, bell pepper, and garlic in olive oil until transparent. Combine the meat and onion mixture. Add pureed tomatoes, water, bay leaf, and Tabasco™. Simmer for 4-5 hours. Thirty minutes before done, add mushrooms.

Colonel Henry G. Casey,
as told by Sandy Riney
Las Piedras Ranch
Real County, Texas

Those who watch Butch's PBS TV Show wonder who he is cooking all that food for 'cause he always eats alone. After the camera stops rolling, though, the crew members anxiously dig in to the grub as it comes out of the "kitchen"
Fall 1999
Penny Welch Photo

Pasta and Meat Balls

Make the meatballs at home for a quick camp meal when campers or hunters are tired, cold, and hungry.

Use 2-3 pounds of Italian sausage without adding any ingredients. Get a big pot of water boiling. Roll the meatballs between your palms about the size of tennis balls. Drop in boiling water and cook until they float. Drain and cool.

Quick Spaghetti Sauce

This sauce also can be made ahead of time and frozen. Get it out in the morning to thaw for dinner. The first person back to camp puts the sauce in a Dutch oven and sets it on the wood stove or a low heat to start warming it up for dinner.

Ingredients:

5-6 cloves garlic
3 Tbsp. olive oil
2 large cans tomato sauce
2 medium cans tomato paste
2 large cans stewed tomatoes
1 cup red wine
Favorite Italian seasonings
Salt and pepper, as desired

Sauté garlic in olive oil. In a large sauce pan or 12 " Dutch oven, put the tomato sauce, tomato paste and tomatoes. Rinse the cans with some of the red wine and water and add to the mixture. Add the rest of the wine to the sauce, along with the garlic and olive oil. Simmer for about an hour, then add meatballs and continue to simmer until meatballs are thoroughly heated.

Boil your favorite pasta according to package directions. I like to use vegetable rotelli or garden rotini for this dish. Drain. Serve the sauce and meatballs over the pasta. Sprinkle Parmesan or Romano cheese over the top. Serve with garlic bread and a green salad.

Wrap knives up in a towel. Don't let them rattle around with your other kitchen utensils. They stay sharper longer and you lessen the risk of cutting your hand when reaching for something else.

──── Musselshell White-Tail Feast ────

Ingredients:

1 White-tail hind quarter, about 6-8 lbs.,
     boneless or bone in
6 cloves garlic, slivered
6 cloves garlic, diced
1/3 cup olive oil
2 cups red wine
8-10 red potatoes, washed
1 ½ cups carrots, sliced into 1 ½" pieces
4-6 ribs celery, cut into 1" chunks
2-3 medium onions, quartered
Pepper/other seasonings, if desired

Pierce the hind quarter and insert pieces of the slivered garlic. Season the meat with pepper and other seasonings. Heat olive oil in a 14" deep Dutch oven, and add the diced garlic. Brown the hind quarter in the olive oil and garlic, turning to brown all sides and the ends. Add the wine and cover the Dutch oven. Place DO in a firepan with 8-10 briquets under the oven and 20-25 briquets on the top. Cook for 2-3 hours, depending upon the size of the hind quarter. Add all the vegetables, and continue to cook for another 45-60 minutes. Additional liquid may need to be added, and charcoal may need to be refreshed to complete cooking.

I made this for the first night of "deer camp" one year when a group of us hunted and camped near Musselshell Guard Station east of Weippe, Idaho. The guys were suitably impressed.

Jambalaya

Ingredients:

1 lb. kielbasa sausage, cut into 1" chunks
1 lb. chicken tenders
1/3 cup vegetable oil
1 cup chopped onion
Pepper to taste
4 cloves garlic, minced
3 cups water
2 tsp. salt
¼ tsp thyme
¼ tsp. marjoram
2 tsp. Worcestershire sauce
1 ½ cups regular rice
1 can mushrooms

Cook chicken and sausage separately. Cook onion, pepper, and garlic in oil. Add water and seasonings. Simmer for 10 minutes. Add meat and rice. Cover and cook 25 minutes. Add mushrooms and cook 5 more minutes. Use 6-8 briquets under the Dutch oven and 12-14 on top. Stir infrequently.

CAMPFIRE CASH

Campfires evoke memories from anyone who has ever sat around listening or telling stories by nature's own light. It is not uncommon for stories bordering on the bizarre to be told and re-told, but while camped at the river put-in on the Bruneau River in SW Idaho, a truly bizarre story unfolded before our eyes.

Anyone who has ever floated the Bruneau River in Idaho's Owyhee County already knows that a big part of the adventure is just getting there! Mile after mile of rutted, kidney-jarring road across a seemingly endless plateau of sagebrush erodes the patience of all in the party. Suddenly what moments before appeared to be a sea of sagebrush is parted by the Bruneau River Canyon, just as the Red Sea parted for Moses and his followers in the Bible story! Though the float trip begins on the river, which twinkles at the canyon bottom, the adventure by road is not yet ended! Now the road descends through a lava escarpment. Chiseled and blasted from solid rock, this road challenges any who dare drop off the canyon rim! Rusted, burned-out hulks lying among the jumbled rocks below the escarpment bear mute testimony to the fate of careless drivers before us.

After successfully making this first descent, my two pards, Jim Van Ark and Mike Brogliatti, and I watched our shuttle drivers attain the rim before starting to rig our boats. We had two days to burn while waiting for the rest of our party to descend the Jarbridge River in canoes and a kayak to where we were. The Jarbridge enters the Bruneau about a mile upstream from the put-in. We pitched our camp near an old bridge that is no longer safe for vehicles to cross. After getting the boats rigged, we checked out nearby Indian Hot Springs and rustled up some firewood for camp. Rather than set up a firepan, I chose to grill our elk steaks over an open fire in a rock fire ring made by previous campers. At one point I thought about relocating a couple of rocks in the fire ring to better balance my grill, but managed to get it steady enough that it wasn't worth the bother. But because I didn't move those rocks, I'll never know the answer to a question I ended up asking the next day. That evening the three of us sat around the fire telling stories, remembering other river trips, and wondering how our pards were faring up on the Jarbridge.

The next morning after rolling out of bed, we immediately congregated around the fire again to ward off the late April chill. After warming my bones, I headed to Indian Hot Springs for a soak and a bath. Jim Van Ark followed minutes later taking photos. As an aside, it was at this time that Jim took the photo of me in the bathtub that appears on the back cover of this book.

When camping, most folks expect some privacy or solitude as part of a camping experience. While camped at the Bruneau River put-in at the end of a dead end road, which almost defies description, 'isolation' better defines our campsite! Being mid-week and early in the floating season, we were not expecting to see anyone else that morning as we sat around drinking coffee. All of a sudden we heard a vehicle approaching and figured another party of floaters were coming in. For a couple of minutes before the rig came into view it almost sounded like an off road motorcycle. In all my years of patrolling and driving back roads in Idaho and other western states imagine my surprise when a two-wheel drive sedan of foreign manufacture came into view.

Our surprise only increased when two fellows, one in his twenties and the other middle-aged got out of the car. Surprise turned to apprehension as these two characters approached us. Had we been in a movie theater I would've thought two characters from "Deliverance" had come to life. My officer safety training kicked in as both guys began to advance after just saying 'Hi'! The older fellow stopped when he reached the fire ring and bent down and rolled over one of the rocks. From underneath the rock he picked up a wad of bills folded in half. Even with a twenty-pound river rock setting on them this wad of bills was almost two inches thick. Before he pocketed the money I could see only the bill on the outside of the roll and it was larger than a twenty!

After backing off a couple of steps the older guy said, "We left this here last weekend and decided to come back and see if it was still here!" He went on to tell us they'd been camped where we were and had hid their money under the rock before walking up to the mouth of the Jarbridge to do some prospecting. Even though I knew it to be a tacky question, I asked how much money was in the roll. He replied, "Just some pocket change." Pocket change my foot! Even if they were all one-dollar bills, these two guys had a bit more than pocket change hidden under that rock! I guess even in the woods folks hide their valuables in odd places! Although a bit bizarre but true, I still tell this one around the fire!

Spicy Italian Red
Beans and Rice

Ingredients:

8 oz. Italian sausage
½ cup chopped onion
½ cup chopped red bell pepper
½ cup chopped green bell pepper
2 cloves garlic, minced
1 can kidney beans, undrained
1 can pinto beans, undrained
1 can Italian tomato soup; or,
1 can tomato soup
1 Tbsp. Italian seasoning
½ cup salsa, medium

Brown sausage and drain. Add onion, peppers and garlic. Cook until tender. Stir in beans, soup and salsa. At home, reduce to low and simmer 15 minutes. In camp, prepare in a Dutch oven. Cover and set the Dutch in the firepan with 6-8 briquets underneath and 14-16 on the lid and cook for about 15 minutes. Spoon over cooked rice. Serves 4.

Bill Beck
Charlotte, North Carolina

CeeDub w/ Sis in Owyhee Co. Spring 1992
Rob Brazie Photo

Rock Salt Prime Rib

Ingredients:

5-7 lb. prime rib, boneless
3-4 Tbsp. coarse ground pepper
2-3 tsp. garlic powder
2 tsp ground rosemary
10-12 lbs. non-iodized rock salt

Place about 1 1/2 inches of rock salt in the bottom of a deep 14" Dutch oven. Mix the pepper, garlic powder, and rosemary together. Rub this mixture onto the prime rib, thoroughly patting in the spices onto the meat. Place the seasoned meat onto the bed of rock salt. Completely cover the entire prime rib with rock salt with about an inch of rock salt on the top of the roast. Place the Dutch oven on the firepan with 12-14 briquets on the bottom and 12-14 briquets on the lid. Cook for about 1 1/2 hours for a medium roast. Take off the heat and let sit for 10-15 minutes, then pull prime rib out of the rock salt. Let the meat rest for a few minutes before slicing. Scrape off excess seasoning. Slice and serve. Horseradish sauce may be added as a garnishment for the prime rib. Cook longer for well done, or cut cooking time for rare.

Pork or Chicken Bake

Ingredients:

4-6 loin pork chops or
        pieces of boneless chicken
1 cup white wine, water, or chicken broth
16 oz. Russian dressing
8 oz. apricot-pineapple jam
1 envelope onion soup mix

Place a wire rack in a Dutch oven and arrange meat pieces on the rack. Pour white wine, water, or chicken broth in the bottom of the Dutch. Mix dressing, jam, and soup mix. Pour over meat. Bake with 8-10 briquets underneath the Dutch oven and 15 or so on the lid, or at 350 degrees in the oven. Bake for about an hour. Serve on bed of rice.

This simple dish is a great main dish when you're in a hurry. For variety try a French or Catalina dressing.

Stuffed Flank Steak

Ingredients:

2 flank steaks
1 cup bread crumbs
1/4 green pepper, chopped fine
1/4 cup celery, chopped fine
1/4 cup onion, chopped fine
2 Tbsp. parsley flakes
Salt/pepper/sage
1/4 cup olive oil or vegetable oil
6 cloves garlic, minced
1 1/2 cups red wine or beef bouillon

Mix bread crumbs, chopped peppers, celery, onion, parsley flakes, and seasonings in a bowl. Use one half mixture for each flank steak. Spreak out steak and spoon on 1/2 of the dry mixture on dry steak. Roll steak lengthwise. Skewer with toothpicks. Halve steaks, if desired. Brown stuffed flank steaks in olive oil and garlic, turning carefully. When brown, add red wine or bouillon and bake in moderate heat for two hours, using 6-8 briquets on the bottom of the Dutch oven and 15-18 briquets on the lid. Add fresh charcoal as needed.

Stuffed Acorn Squash

Ingredients:

> 3 acorn squash
> 3/4 lb. hamburger, mixed with sausage optional
> 1/2 onion, chopped
> 1/2 green pepper, chopped fine
> 3 cloves garlic minced, or garlic powder equivalent
> 4 Tbsp. Worcestershire sauce
> Salt/pepper/hot pepper sauce, as desired
> Tomato ketchup, optional
> 1 slice bacon, diced
> Water for cooking liquid

Cut the top off the squash and clean out the inside. Trim the bottom slightly so that it will sit flat on the bottom of a Dutch, or on a rack. Mix the hamburger and other ingredients in a separate bowl. Spoon the meat loaf filling into the squash, filling above the top. Place diced bacon on the top. Place the filled squash in a 12 " Dutch oven, or on a rack in a 12 " Dutch oven. Add liquid to steam and cook the stuffed squash. Bake for approximately 1 hour, using 5-7 briquets on the bottom, and 15-20 briquets on the lid. Serves 3.

This recipe makes a great casserole dish, but includes a vegetable to balance the meal.

Words of Wisdom

When you pick a spot for your campfire pay attention to the prevailing winds around camp. Don't pitch tents downwind, especially those made with nylon or other synthetics, as a single spark blown from a campfire can ignite them.

Roast Leg of Lamb

Ingredients:

4-5 lb. leg of lamb
8 cloves garlic, slivered
Salt/pepper/seasonings to taste
1/4 cup olive oil
4 cloves garlic, minced
1-1 1/2 cups red wine or other cooking liquid
8-12 red potatoes, depending on size
3 celery ribs, cut into 1" pieces
4 carrots, cleaned and cut into 1" piece
4-6 boiling onions, or 2 small onions quartered
1 cup brussels sprouts, optional

Pierce the leg of lamb in various places and insert the slivers of garlic. Season roast with salt, pepper, and other seasonings. Heat olive oil in 12" or 14" deep Dutch oven. Add minced garlic when hot. Brown roast on all sides in the olive oil and garlic. When brown, add red wine or cooking liquid. About every 15 minutes, brush the horseradish glaze, recipe follows, over the roast. Cook for about 1 hour, until roast is beginning to get tender, using 8-10 briquets under the Dutch oven, and 18-20 on the lid.

Remove lid and add all the vegetables. Cook another 20-25 minutes until vegetables are done. Remove the roast, let it rest for a few minutes, slice and serve. Use the remaining glaze as a garnishment.

Honey Horseradish Glaze

6-8 oz. creamy horseradish
3/4-1 cup honey

Heat the creamy horseradish and honey in a separate pan, mixing thoroughly, until it boils. Remove from heat. Baste or brush the roast with the glaze while roast is cooking about every 15 minutes.

Stuffed Peppers

Ingredients:

> 4-6 bell peppers, tops cut off and cleaned
> 1-1/2 lbs. hamburger meat
> ½ onion, diced
> 3 green onions, diced
> 1 can tomato sauce
> 2 eggs
> Salt/pepper/garlic powder

Mix all the ingredients and stuff the peppers. Bake covered at 350 degrees for one hour.

Marie Mathis
Somerville, Texas

Marie makes this at home or as a special at the Old Depot Antiques Restaurant in Round Top, Texas. For a Dutch oven dinner, place the stuffed peppers in a 12" DO and add one cup water or broth. Bake for 40 minutes with 8 briquets underneath and 18-20 on top.

Roast Pork with Sweet and Sour Sauce

Ingredients:

> 4 –1 lb. pork roasts, or chops
> ¼ cup olive oil
> 2 cups sugar
> 1 cup white distilled vinegar
> 2 Tbsp. chopped green pepper
> 1 cup water
> 1 tsp. salt
> 4 Tbsp. cornstarch
> 2 Tbsp. water
> 2 tsp. paprika
> 1 tbsp parsley

Place the pork roasts or chops in a Dutch oven and brown in the olive oil. To make the sauce, combine sugar, vinegar, green pepper, water, and salt. Simmer for 5 minutes. Thicken with the cornstarch dissolved in water. Add the paprika and parsley. Pour the sauce over the browned pork and bake at 300 degrees for about 2 ½ hours, basting occasionally, using 4 briquets under the Dutch oven and 12-14 on the lid. The charcoal will need to be freshened periodically to complete cooking.

———————— White-Tail Stir Fry ————————

Ingredients:

> 1-2 lbs. round steaks, cut into 1" strips
> Peanut oil
> 2-3 cloves garlic, finely minced
> 2 Tbsp. minced ginger
> 1-2 tsp. soy sauce
> 1 onion, diced
> 1/2 cup chopped celery
> 1/2 red pepper, diced
> 1/2 green pepper, diced
> 2 cups cauliflower florets
> 2 cups broccoli florets
> 1 cup carrots sliced into ¼" pieces
> 1 cup cabbage, chunked into large pieces
> 1 cup mushrooms, sliced

Set 12" Dutch oven on camp stove on high. Add peanut oil. Fry the garlic and ginger to flavor the oil, then remove them from the oil and set aside. Garlic and ginger may be added back into the vegetables later, if desired. Add the meat and quickly fry for about 3-5 minutes, until nearly done. Remove, and set aside. Add the soy sauce and the veggies one at a time to the Dutch, starting with the ones that take the longest to cook and ending with the cabbage and mushrooms. Add the meat back into the mixture to heat thoroughly and finish cooking. Serve over a bed of rice.

DESSERTS

Where Do You Buy Scratch

As a general practice, by accident or design, I use very few mixes and pre-packaged items. Maybe that is partly because of the way I was brought up. But I also actually enjoy making things the old-fashioned way with basic ingredients. For some reason, I think it tastes better. However, if my students want to use mixes for ease and convenience while learning to cook in Dutch ovens, or time is a factor, I encourage the use of items already prepared. There's no need to make things more complicated than necessary.

Along those lines, I recently ran across the following story that depicts this dilemna of a beginning cook.

• • • • • • • • • • • • • • • • • • •

My mother never let me help much in the kitchen. As a result my cooking ability was practically non-existent when I got married. But I did remember mother mentioning to her friends that she made cakes, pies, and other things from scratch.

With mother's delicious cakes in mind, my first trip to the supermarket was to buy some scratch. I found the aisles that read "baking items". I spent a good fifteen minutes looking at everything from vegetable oil, sugar, flour, and chocolate without ever seeing a sign of scratch. I was sure it wouldn't be with pickles or meat. I asked a clerk if they carried scratch. He looked at me kind of funny and finally said, "You'll have to go to the store on the corner." When I got there, it turned out to be a feed store. I thought it rather strange, but I decided cakes were feed. I asked the clerk, "Do you have scratch?" He asked me how much I wanted. I suggested a pound or two. His reply was, "How many chickens do you have? It only comes in 20 pound bags." I really didn't understand why he mentioned chickens, but I had heard my mother say she made chicken casserole from scratch, so I bought 20 pounds and hurried home.

My next problem was to find a recipe calling for scratch. I went through every single page of my lovely "Better Homes and Garden Cookbook" given to us as a wedding gift, looking for a recipe calling for scratch. There I was with 20 pounds of scratch and no recipe.

When I opened the scratch, I had doubts that a beautiful fluffy cake would ever result from such a hard-looking ingredient. I hoped with the addition of liquids and heat, the result would be successful. I had no need to mention my problem to my husband as he suggested very early in our marriage that he liked to cook and would gladly take over any time.

One day he made a pie and when I told him how good it was, he said he made it from scratch. That assured me it could be done. Being a new bride is scary and when I found out he made pies and cakes and even lemon pudding from scratch….. Well, if he made all those things from scratch, I was sure he had 20 pounds also. But I couldn't find where he stored it. I checked my supply; it was still full. At this point I was ready to give up because all the people knew about scratchy except me.

I decided to try a different approach. One day when my husband was not doing anything, I said, "Honey, I wish you would bake a cake." He got out the flour, sugar, eggs, milk and shortening, but not a sign of scratch. I watched him blend it all together, pour it into a pan and slide it into the oven to bake. An hour later as we were eating the cake, I looked at him and smiled and said, "Honey, why don't we raise a few chickens?"

- Author Unknown

—— Basque Blackberry Cobbler ——

Ingredients:

6 oz. cream cheese
2 cubes butter
2 cups flour
Pinch of salt
4 cups berries
1/2 cup sugar
1/2 teaspoon nutmeg
1 teaspoon cinnamon
1 teaspoon lemon or lime juice
1/2 cup flour
2 tablespoons melted butter

For pastry, cut the cream cheese and butter into flour and salt. Form soft dough into ball and chill. Pour berries into 12" Dutch oven and sprinkle with sugar, nutmeg, cinnamon, and juice. Sprinkle with flour and drip melted butter over the top of fruit. Roll well-chilled pastry dough to about 11" circle. Carefully place the crust over the berries. Use 5-6 briquets under the Dutch oven and load the lid with 25 briquets. Bake for 45 minutes.

Dave McGonigal
Idaho Fish & Game
Boise, Idaho

Dave, a fellow game warden, is one of the most accomplished cooks I've ever met. His name is Irish, but the other side of Dave's family tree has its roots in the Basque provinces of Spain. Growing up on the family sheep ranch in Idaho's Wood River Valley influenced Dave to become a camp cook in his own right. When time came for college, Dave paid his way through school by becoming a restaurant cook/chef. Whenever you see a recipe with Dave's name on it, you can bet you're at the top of the list.

Baked Bananas

Ingredients:

Fresh bananas
Milk chocolate bars
Miniature marshmallows
Aluminum foil for wrapping

Make about a 10 inch square of aluminum for each banana. Place each banana on a piece of foil. Slit the skin of each banana on the side that is curved and peel skin away from the banana. Tuck chocolate pieces, as many as will fit, on each side of the banana, between the banana and the skin. Fill in the additional space with marshmallows. Bunch up the foil around the banana, also covering the banana, making a boat for the banana. Put the bananas in a Dutch oven with 4-5 briquets on the bottom and 15 on top, and bake for 10-15 minutes.

George Hirsch, a fellow PBS cook from New York specializing in grill cooking, showed me this recipe when we both appeared at a festival at Itchycoo Park '99, near Manchester, Tennessee. They are quick to fix and will satisfy the "sweet tooth" of campers anytime.

Butch & George Hirsch
Penny Welch Photo

Blackberry Cake

Ingredients:

1 yellow or white cake mix
2 cups blackberries, fresh or frozen
Half and half, rather than water

Follow directions on the box, adding suggested ingredients such as eggs and salad oil. However, instead of adding water as the liquid, add half and half in the quantity specified. Stir ingredients in a large bowl until thoroughly blended. Pour into a 12" Dutch oven. Drop blackberries into batter. Bake according to directions on the mix, using 5-6 briquets under the oven and 20-25 on the lid, baking for 30-40 minutes. Because half and half is used rather than water, the cake turns out very rich and much heavier. Very good!

We make this with blackberries because they are so plentiful around our house. Any fresh berries will work, even other fresh fruits work well. But be advised that when I tried this with strawberries, they didn't look very appetizing.

Cee Dub's Quick Fruit Cobbler

Mix at home in a self-sealing plastic bag:

2 cups flour
2 Tbsp. baking powder
Pinch of salt

At camp, mix dry ingredients with:

1 1/3 cups milk
¼ cup vegetable oil

Spread dough mixture into a 12" Dutch oven. Drop spoonfuls of your favorite store-bought pie filling on top. Bake with 4-5 briquets underneath and 20-25 on the lid for 30-40 minutes. Rotate the Dutch a couple of times to avoid hot spots.

Cherry Chocolate
Dump Cake

Ingredients:

2 cans cherry pie filling
1 chocolate cake mix
  (the kind with pudding in the mix)
1-20 oz. bottle of cherry flavored carbonated soda

Place cans of pie filling in the bottom of a 12" Dutch oven. Sprinkle cake mix over the fruit filling. Gently pour the carbonated soda over the cake mix. Cover and bake using 5-6 briquets under the Dutch oven, 20 on the outside rim of the lid and 3-4 in the middle of the lid. Bake 35-45 minutes. The dessert can be topped with ice cream or whipped cream for an added treat.

The first time someone tastes "dump cake" they can't believe the recipe calls for only three ingredients: 2 cans of fruit, 1 cake mix with pudding in the mix, and a 20 ounce bottle of soda. The recipe was made for novice DO cooks. There is no measuring, no complicated preparation, and a very tasty dessert results. Only your imagination limits the combinations that can be created by using different fruits, different flavors of cake mix, and different flavors of soda.

NOTE - To make dump cake with fresh fruit, you need one additional ingredient. Sprinkle one-half cup flour over the fruit to act as a thickener.

Cee Dub & Jack packing home some venison 1989
C.W. Welch Photo Collection

Brownies

Ingredients:

1 packaged brownie mix
1/2 cup chopped nuts

Follow directions on the box, adding suggested ingredients such as eggs and liquid. Stir ingredients in a bowl until thoroughly blended, according to package instructions. Pour into a 12" Dutch oven. Sprinkle chopped nuts over top of batter. Bake according to directions on the mix, using 5-6 briquets under the oven and 20-25 on the lid, baking for approximately 30-40 minutes.

Try making these for the kids as a snack. Better yet, teach them how to make their own brownies. This is a simple recipe that is a great way to recruit a cook's helper.

Mama's Shortcake

Ingredients:

1 cup flour
2 tsp. baking powder
Pinch of salt
¾ cup sugar
Shortening, size of an egg
1 egg
Milk to moisten

Sift flour, baking powder and salt. Cream sugar and shortening; and beat in the egg. Beat flour mixture slowly into sugar mixture, and alternate with enough milk to barely moisten the batter. Bake in a 9 inch square pan at 350 degrees for 20-25 minutes.

Sandy Riney
Las Piedras Ranch
Real County, Texas

Sweet Potato Pie

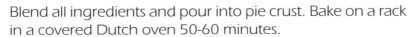

Ingredients:

2 cups baked sweet potatoes
2 eggs, beaten
1 ¼ cups milk
¾ cup sugar
½ tsp. salt
½ tsp. cinnamon
½ tsp. nutmeg
2 Tbsp. rum
4 Tbsp. butter, softened or melted
9" pie crust

Blend all ingredients and pour into pie crust. Bake on a rack in a covered Dutch oven 50-60 minutes.

Bill Beck
Charlotte, North Carolina

Fresh Peach Cobbler

Ingredients: Fruit Mixture

6 cups peaches, peeled and sliced
3/4 cup honey
1/4 cup flour
1/2 tsp. nutmeg
1/2 tsp. cinnamon
Dash of salt

Ingredients: Crumb mixture

1 cup flour
3/4 cup rolled oats
1 cup brown sugar
1/2 cup melted butter or margarine
1 tsp. cinnamon

Stir together the fruit mixture and spoon into a 12" Dutch oven. Combine and mix all the ingredients for the crumb mixture. Spread/crumble this over the fruit filling. Set your DO in the firepan with 3-5 briquets underneath and 18-22 on the lid and bake for 45-50 minutes.Serves 8.

——— Words of Wisdom ———

Make a thermos of coffee the night before and place it with a coffee cup next to the cooks bunk. He will get up in a much better humor the next morning.

——— Cherry or Blueberry Cobbler———

Ingredients:

1 can pie filling with liquid
1/3 cup lemon juice
1 Tbsp. tapioca or cornstarch
¼ tsp. salt
1 ½ cups sugar
Splash of vanilla

1 yellow cake mix
½ cup Bisquick®
¼ tsp. salt
1 Tbsp. baking powder

Mix top items together and pour into greased 10" Dutch oven. Mix cake items and sprinkle over fruit filling. Dot with margarine and bake for one hour at 350 degrees or using 5-6 briquets under the Dutch oven and 8-10 on the lid, adding more as needed. Recipe can be doubled using a 12" Dutch oven.

Dan Miller
Grand Junction, Colorado

Cherry Swirl Cake

Ingredients:

1 white or yellow cake mix
Cherry flavored syrup, or other fruit flavor

Follow directions on the box, adding suggested ingredients such as eggs, salad oil, and water. Stir ingredients in a large bowl until thoroughly blended. Pour into a 12" Dutch oven. Drizzle cherry syrup into the batter in a spiral design. Other flavored syrups may be used. Bake according to directions on the mix, using 5-6 briquets under the oven and 20-25 on the lid, baking for 30-40 minutes.

This makes a quick and fairly light dessert; unless, of course, you use the whole bottle of syrup. Another variation is to serve with ice cream or whipped cream.

Words of Wisdom

Take extra precautions when preparing poultry. Wash and disinfect your hands, utensils, and cutting boards before using them again.

Rhubard and/or Strawberry Upside-Down Cake

Ingredients:

1 pkg. yellow or sour cream yellow cake mix
1 cup diced rhubarb and/or strawberries
    (Actually, I like lots more rhubarb to make it
    like a deep dish pie.)
1 ½ cups sugar added to rhubarb
1 cup whipping cream, not whipped

Mix cake according to box directions and pour into a 12"
Dutch oven. Pour fruit mixture evenly over cake mix. Then
pour whipping cream over fruit and cake mix. Bake until
brown, approximately 1 hour, using 5-6 briquets under the
oven and 20-25 on the lid. Cool and turn upside down or
serve as is. Whipped cream on top is excellent.

Mike McLain
Colorado Division of Wildlife

Pen's Pineapple Upside
———————— Dump Cake ————————

Ingredients:

1 white or yellow cake mix
1/4 lb. butter
1 cup brown sugar
1-20 oz. bottle of carbonated lemon-lime soda
1 20 oz. can crushed pineapple

Melt butter and brown sugar in the bottom of a 12" Dutch
oven, and spread evenly over the bottom of the DO. Pour in
undrained pineapple. Sprinkle dry cake mix over the
pineapple. Gently pour carbonated soda over cake mix.
Cover and bake using 5-6 briquets under the Dutch oven,
20 on the outside rim of the lid and 3-4 in the middle of the
lid. Bake 40-50 minutes.

My wife came up with this variation of the basic dump cake
for a river trip with friends down Idaho's Main Salmon River.

LAST WORD

This book is by no means 'The Complete Camp Cookbook"! I couldn't write such a book because it would mean revising it after every camping trip. Camping and camp cooking continue to evolve, as does everything else. However, this book will benefit both the beginning camp cook and those who've spent a fair amount of time cooking for hungry campers. If you've read this far you've figured out my philosophy extends beyond just having good grub in camp. I started out camping with my folks and sisters as a little kid in SE Idaho. As an adult my profession plus my interest in white water rafting and horse packing allowed me to camp over a good part of Idaho and other western states as well. Whether solo camping or camping as part of a group, I enjoy spending time outdoors!

My tenure as a conservation officer also influenced the content of this book. I've witnessed folks feeling miserable because they didn't have the proper gear or the knowledge and information needed when they ventured beyond roads end. I also feel obligated to do my part in educating folks about more mundane things like water and garbage, and to pass along tips that make camp life easier. I'm no efficiency expert, but there will always be the easy way and the hard way of doing things, camping and camp cookin' included!

I focused this book on camping and cookin' in camp, but I encourage anyone with an interest in outdoor cooking to try his or her own hand with a Dutch oven. DO cookin' tastes as great on the patio as it does in the back country!

In camp the cook tent or campfire usually ends up being the social center where folks gather to both start a new day and to say goodnight. The good times in between are just part of the reason we all go camping. In the physical sense it takes wood to fuel a campfire; but on the other hand, I've never sat next to a campfire that wasn't in part fueled with memories. I hope you enjoyed reading the stories, trying the recipes, and that the next time you're sitting around a campfire you take the time to remember your pards, both past and present!

C.W. "Butch" Welch
March 2000

More from Cee Dub!

Visit our Website at *ceedubs.com*!

BOOKS AND TAPES

If you have questions or wish to order additional copies of books, just contact us via the World Wide Web. Copies of both of Cee Dub's cookbooks, as well as a 65 minute VHS 'How-To' Video Tape are all available. Do you need a personally autographed book for the camp cook in your life? Just let us know with your order and we'll be happy to oblige. Also, you can contact Cee Dub by e-mail for the answers to your camp cooking questions!

* *Cee Dub's Dutch Oven and other Camp Cookin'* - $18.95

* ***More*** *Cee Dub's Dutch Oven and Other Camp Cookin'* - $18.95

* *Dutch Oven & Camp Cooking - VHS video tape (65 min)* - $19.95

Any order of more than one book or tape receives one dollar off each additional item.

Shipping/Handling is $4.50 for first item, plus $1.50 for each additional item by UPS or Priority mail. Orders of five or more items are shipped UPS Ground, pre-paid. Allow 2-3 weeks for delivery.

COOKING EQUIPMENT AND SUPPLIES

Cee Dub also carries a full line of Dutch oven equipment. Listed below are some, but not all, of the items we carry. New items are added frequently!

Lodge Dutch ovens, accessories, and cooking equipment

USFS approved **Firepans** - Great for camping, patio cooking, and tailgate parties

Cooking Tables - great for patio as well as camp

Lid Lifters, **Lid Stands**, Dutch oven **Tote Bags**, Kitchen **Utensil Organizers**

Propane Cook Stoves, Water Purification Systems, Portable Toilets

Folding Cook Tables with food grade cutting board tops. For food preparation they can't be beat! Built with longer legs, they eliminate back strain caused from bending over conventional camp tables

COOKING CLINICS

During the summers Cee Dub conducts several cooking clinics specializing in hands-on Dutch oven cooking techniques. The clinics usually begin on Thursday evenings and end Sunday mornings, and are *limited to 12 participants per clinic*. Featured guest instructors, as available, participate, as well. The schedule and other details of the clinics are posted on the Website.

Check our Web Site frequently for new additions to our product line and upcoming events!

WE WOULD ENJOY HEARING FROM YOU !!!!!

Cee Dub serves up the grub for anxious food sampler! May, 1998.   Penny Welch Photo

Publisher's Note

As publisher of Cee Dub's second Dutch oven cookbook, I want to give you some insight into it's evolution from conception to finished manuscript. Butch and I began collecting recipes and story ideas before we were married in 1998. In our travels around the country and while shooting his Public Television Series, *Dutch Oven and Camp Cooking,* we looked for recipes which pleased the taste buds but didn't require extraordinary ingredients or preparation. Having spent twenty-one years as a Conservation Officer for IDF&G, Butch has spent more time than most camp cooking. He knows the value of nutritious meals in camp and from experience how to quickly and easily prepare them. The recipes we've included were selected based on those criteria. Since we began the book, many a meal, both at home and in camp, fell into the R & D category. Research & Dinner! Hopefully you will enjoy the results of our research as much as we did gathering data!

The logo for Back Country Press comes from a print of Bill Pogue, a co-worker of Butch's who lost his life in the line of duty in 1981. Only after his death did most people learn of Bill's artistic ability. Among Bill's favorite subjects were the cowboys of Owyhee County in SW Idaho. I would like to thank Bill's widow, Dee, and the rest of the Pogue family for allowing its use.

Notes